A FACING HISTORY AND OURSELVES PUBLICATION

CHOOSING TO PARTICIPATE »
REVISED EDITION

FACING
HISTORY
AND
OURSELVES

Facing History and Ourselves is an international educational and professional development organization whose mission is to engage students of diverse backgrounds in an examination of racism, prejudice, and antisemitism in order to promote the development of a more humane and informed citizenry. By studying the historical development of the Holocaust and other examples of genocide, students make the essential connection between history and the moral choices they confront in their own lives. For more information about Facing History and Ourselves, please visit our website at *www.facinghistory.org.*

Cover art photos: (top, left to right): *Nicholas Winton* photo courtesy of Press Association; *Marian Anderson* photo courtesy of Getty Images; *Scream* courtesy of Will Counts Collection: Indiana University Archives; (bottom) *Citizens Protesting Anti-semitic Acts, Billings, MT* courtesy of Howard Greenberg Gallery. Copyright © by Frédéric Brenner.

To order classroom copies, please fax a purchase order to 617-232-0281 or call 617-232-1595 to place a phone order. To download a PDF of this guide free-of-charge, please visit *www.choosingtoparticipate.org.*

ISBN-13: 978-0-9798440-8-9

Facing History and Ourselves Headquarters
16 Hurd Road
Brookline, MA 02445-6919

FACING
HISTORY
AND
OURSELVES

ABOUT FACING HISTORY AND OURSELVES

Facing History and Ourselves is a nonprofit educational organization whose mission is to engage students of diverse backgrounds in an examination of racism, prejudice, and antisemitism in order to promote a more humane and informed citizenry. As the name Facing History and Ourselves implies, the organization helps teachers and their students make the essential connections between history and the moral choices they confront in their own lives, and offers a framework and a vocabulary for analyzing the meaning and responsibility of citizenship and the tools to recognize bigotry and indifference in their own worlds. Through a rigorous examination of the failure of democracy in Germany during the 1920s and '30s and the steps leading to the Holocaust, along with other examples of hatred, collective violence, and genocide in the past century, Facing History and Ourselves provides educators with tools for teaching history and ethics, and for helping their students learn to combat prejudice with compassion, indifference with participation, myth and misinformation with knowledge.

Believing that no classroom exists in isolation, Facing History and Ourselves offers programs and materials to a broad audience of students, parents, teachers, civic leaders, and all of those who play a role in the education of young people. Through significant higher education partnerships, Facing History and Ourselves also reaches and impacts teachers before they enter their classrooms.

By studying the choices that led to critical episodes in history, students learn how issues of identity and membership, ethics and judgment have meaning today and in the future. Facing History and Ourselves' resource books provide a meticulously researched yet flexible structure for examining complex events and ideas. Educators can select appropriate readings and draw on additional resources available online or from our comprehensive lending library.

Our foundational resource book, *Facing History and Ourselves: Holocaust and Human Behavior*, embodies a sequence of study that begins with identity—first individual identity and then group and national identities, with their definitions of membership. From there the program examines the failure of democracy in Germany and the steps leading to the Holocaust—

the most documented case of twentieth-century indifference, de-humanization, hatred, racism, antisemitism, and mass murder. It goes on to explore difficult questions of judgment, memory, and legacy, and the necessity for responsible participation to prevent injustice. Facing History and Ourselves then returns to the theme of civic participation to examine stories of individuals, groups, and nations who have worked to build just and inclusive communities and whose stories illuminate the courage, compassion, and political will that are needed to protect democracy today and in generations to come. Other examples in which civic dilemmas test democracy, such as the Armenian Genocide and the U.S. civil rights movement, expand and deepen the connection between history and the choices we face today and in the future.

Facing History and Ourselves has offices or resource centers in the United States, Canada, and the United Kingdom as well as in-depth partnerships in Rwanda, South Africa, and Northern Ireland. Facing History and Ourselves' outreach is global, with educators trained in more than 80 countries and delivery of our resources through a website accessed worldwide with online content delivery, a program for international fellows, and a set of NGO partnerships. By convening conferences of scholars, theologians, educators, and journalists, Facing History and Ourselves' materials are kept timely, relevant, and responsive to salient issues of global citizenship in the twenty-first century.

For more than 30 years, Facing History and Ourselves has challenged students and educators to connect the complexities of the past to the moral and ethical issues of today. They explore democratic values and consider what it means to exercise one's rights and responsibilities in the service of a more humane and compassionate world. They become aware that "little things are big"—seemingly minor decisions can have a major impact and change the course of history.

For more about Facing History and Ourselves, visit our website at *www.facinghistory.org.*

ACKNOWLEDGMENTS

Facing History and Ourselves extends special gratitude to The Walmart Foundation for lead sponsorship of the national five-city tour of *Choosing to Participate* and the re-release of this book which has been developed to give educators a tool to explore the role of citizenship in democracy. We wish to thank as well the many funders and leaders who are supporting this initiative as it travels nationally.

Creating this project has been a wonderfully collaborative experience at Facing History and Ourselves. There are so many people to thank for their good work on this project: Phyllis Goldstein wrote the original study guide, and Adam Strom wrote new readings for this revision. Terry Tollefson helped update the Preface, and Margot Stern Strom, Marty Sleeper, and Marc Skvirsky were a thoughtful and supportive editorial team. A special thanks is extended to Sarah Haacke who oversees the *Choosing to Participate* initiative, and Emma Smizik who coordinates countless details for the project. Catherine O'Keefe, Rachel Murray, Jenifer Snow, Maria Hill, and Ilana Klarman all worked hard to bring this book together. We would also like to thank Josephine Roccuzzo for her copy-editing, The Herman Lewis Design Syndicate for their production work, and Tom Beckham for his work on the cover design.

ACCESS FACING HISTORY AND OURSELVES CONTENT ONLINE

Engage students with our dynamic teaching resources.

FACING TODAY links current events to important civic and historical themes.
facinghistory.org/facingtoday

CHOOSINGTOPARTICIPATE.ORG engages students by using cutting-edge technology aimed at inspiring participation in the community.

BE THE CHANGE connects students with stories of community upstanders through a journey meant to engage the civic participant in all of us.
facinghistory.org/bethechange

FACINGHISTORY.ORG helps classrooms and communities link the past to moral choices today.

FACING
HISTORY
AND
OURSELVES

CONTENTS

PREFACE

By Terry Tollefson, Facing History and Ourselves staff member

Choosing to Participate focuses on civic choices—the decisions people make about themselves and others in their community, nation, and world. The choices people make, both large and small, may not seem important at the time, but little by little they shape us as individuals and responsible global citizens.

The legacies of the twentieth century include the horrors of humiliation, dehumanization, discrimination, and genocide. These legacies continue to fuel confrontations among people all over the world, and signals from the early twenty-first century are that ethnic and religious intolerance are once again leading to violence around the globe. The challenge for educators is to create settings that can help young people develop as thoughtful, caring, compassionate, and responsible citizens. These conversations need to be informed by history so that young people can be better prepared to participate in practices and policies that prevent violence and promote peace. If education is truly to be a preparation for life, then these are the lessons that cannot go untaught.

Facing History and Ourselves intends for *Choosing to Participate* to be a catalyst for conversation about how we treat each other, how we should live together, and what our choices mean. The key challenge is to think deeply about what democracy really means, and what it asks of each of us. Democracy is a fragile enterprise and can only remain vital through the active, thoughtful, and responsible participation of its people. Education for citizenship means encouraging each of us to recognize that our participation matters.

Choosing to Participate grew out of our early experience in Facing History and Ourselves classrooms when, after learning about the failure of democracy and the steps that led to the Holocaust, students asked, *How can I make a positive difference in the world?* Facing History and Ourselves is a sequence of study that begins with an examination of self and others, first by exploring individual identity and group identities, and then examining the motivations and choices that led to genocide and collective violence. The study goes on to explore difficult questions of judgment, memory, and legacy, and the necessity for responsible participation to prevent injustice.

Throughout the Facing History and Ourselves journey into history and ethics, students are inspired by individuals and groups whose stories illuminate the courage, initiative, and compassion that are needed to protect democracy and human rights today and in generations to come. By ending with stories of civic participation, the Facing History and Ourselves journey helps teachers and students think about what it means to be good citizens in their schools, their neighborhoods, their nation, and around the world.

The stories in this book will engage young people as they begin to understand that the choices they make as members of a civic society matter to themselves, their communities, and to future generations.

Over 30 years of experiences has demonstrated that Facing History and Ourselves can add a critical cognitive component to service learning by examining and highlighting the stories of people from diverse backgrounds who tried to confront some of the serious social issues of their time. These individuals and groups worked during their lifetime to create positive change and leave a legacy for the next generation. Among these lessons are that civilized society, and democracy in particular, must be worked at if it is to be preserved, and in order to do this we must understand our relationship to the events unfolding around us and our responsibility for our part in them.

Democracy requires the active engagement of its citizens. Equipping young people with the knowledge, skills, and dispositions necessary for civic engagement is central to this task. This book will continue to inspire students as they grow into tomorrow's leaders.

One Facing History student explained, "If one by one, hundreds of children learn the evils of hatred in history, then learn to face and change that history in their own world through art, language, and service and begin to build communities of educated, committed citizens, who is to say that Facing History cannot be the catalyst for an end to prejudice, violence, and injustice?" The educator's most important task—to shape a humane, informed citizenry—has never been more urgent or more vital to the preservation of democratic values and human rights.

Democracy: A Work in Progress

Democracy is a work in progress. It is shaped by the choices ordinary people make about themselves and others. Although those choices may not seem important at the time, little by little, they define an individual, create a community, and ultimately forge a nation.

In a democracy, the decisions people make are tested through conversation, discussion, and debate. It is a process that can only be carried out in what Judge Learned Hand once called "the spirit of liberty." He defined it as the spirit "which is not too sure it is right," the spirit "which seeks to understand the minds of other men and women . . .[and] weighs their interests alongside its own without bias."[1]

That spirit is reflected in the Declaration of Independence. It expresses the ideals of the American people. The document boldly states that all people are "created equal." They also have an "inalienable right" to "life, liberty, and the pursuit of happiness." In 1776, no community in the new nation lived up to those ideals. Over the years, however, many individuals and groups have struggled to bring the nation closer to them. Their efforts often began close to home and gradually expanded to include the entire nation.

The push to end slavery in the United States was one of many movements that began in churches and other small community-based groups. The first successes of these groups were at the local and state levels. In time, they organized nationally and then internationally. The Civil War was fought, at least in part, to advance the democratic ideals they advocated. Although the war ended slavery in the nation, it did not end discrimination.

In 1896, an African American named Homer Plessy challenged in court practices that discriminated against blacks. The case, known as *Plessy v. Ferguson*, went to the Supreme Court. The justices ruled that separate facilities for blacks do not violate the Constitution as long as they are equal to those of whites. The decision permitted the growth of the "Jim Crow" laws—a system of local and state laws that established racial barriers in almost every aspect of life. In many places, black and white Americans could not publicly eat, drink, or travel side by side. Churches, movie theaters, even cemeteries were segregated.

By the early 1900s, writes historian Lerone Bennett, Jr., "America was two nations–one white, one black, separate and unequal." He likens segregation to "a wall, a system, a way of separating people from people." That wall did not go up in a single day. It was built–"brick by brick, bill by bill, fear by fear."[2] In the 1940s and early 1950s, when Marian Wright Edelman was growing up in South Carolina, that wall seemed almost impenetrable. Her parents and other adults in the black community were too vulnerable to challenge segregation directly. Instead, they directed their efforts to resisting its effects so that their children never lost hope. Edelman recalls:

> The church was a hub of Black children's social existence, and caring Black adults were buffers against the segregated and hostile outside world that told us we weren't important. But our parents said it wasn't so, our teachers said it wasn't so, and our preachers said it wasn't so. The message of my racially segregated childhood was clear: let no man or woman look down on you, and look down on no man or woman.

> We couldn't play in public playgrounds or sit at drugstore lunch counters and order a Coke, so Daddy built a playground and canteen behind the church. In fact, whenever he saw a need, he tried to respond. There were no Black homes for the aged in South Carolina, so he began one across the street for which he and Mama and we children cooked and served and cleaned. And we children learned that it was our responsibility to take care of elderly family members and neighbors, and that everyone was our neighbor. . . .

> We learned early what our parents and extended community "parents" valued. Children were taught–not by sermonizing, but by personal example–that nothing was too lowly to do. I remember a debate my parents had when I was eight or nine as to whether I was too young to go with my older brother, Harry, to help clean the bed and bedsores of a very sick, poor woman. I went and learned just how much the smallest helping hands and kindness can mean to a person in need. . . .

> I was fourteen years old the night my daddy died. He had holes in his shoes but two children out of college, one in college, another in divinity school, and a vision he was able to convey to

me as he lay dying in an ambulance that I, a young Black girl, could be and do anything; that race and gender are shadows; and that character, self-discipline, determination, attitude, and service are the substance of life.

I have always believed that I could help change the world because I have been lucky to have adults around me who did—in small and large ways. . . .

I and my brothers and sister might have lost hope—as many young people today have lost hope—except for the stable, caring, attentive adults in our family, school, congregation, civic and political life who struggled with and for us against the obstacles we faced and provided us positive alternatives and the sense of possibility we needed. . . .

My life is one of the countless lives that attest to the vibrancy of the American Dream under circumstances harder than today's. The segregated world of my childhood in the 1940s and 1950s seemed impenetrable. Never could I have envisaged the positive changes I have seen since my youth. But my parents and elders dreamed of them and never lost hope. So neither will I lose hope that America's best self will overcome growing racial and class divisions.[3]

Long before Edelman was born, individuals and groups were challenging segregation in court. Little by little, they broke one legal barrier after another. As a college student, Edelman joined the struggle by demanding laws that protected the rights of all Americans. In 1965, she became the first African American woman to practice law in Mississippi. Over 20 years ago, she founded the Children's Defense Fund, a research and lobbying group devoted to the needs of children.

CONNECTIONS

What choices did adults—both black and white—make about membership and belonging in Edelman's hometown? How did their choices shape both the black and white communities? To what extent did those choices build on the work of earlier generations? What legacy did they leave for generations to come?

The "spirit of liberty," as defined by Justice Learned Hand, was reflected in the efforts of black and white Americans who spoke, wrote, and formed groups in an effort to end segregation. Their right to do these things was protected under the First Amendment to the Constitution. How important was that right in the struggle for equal rights? How did it keep hope alive for Marian Wright Edelman and other African American children?

Author Suzanne Goldsmith writes that "communities are not built of friends, or of groups of people with similar styles and tastes, or even of people who like and understand each other. They are built of people who feel they are part of something that is bigger than themselves: a shared goal or enterprise. . . . To build a community requires only the ability to see value in others; to look at them and see a potential partner in one's enterprise."[4] Sociologist Helen Fein has defined community in terms of a "universe of obligation"—a circle of individuals and groups "toward whom obligations are owed, to whom rules apply, and whose injuries call for [amends]."[5] How are the two definitions alike? How does each relate to Edelman's observations about the community in which she grew up? to what you know about your own community?

The words *community* and *communicate* both come from a Latin word that means "to make public or common." What role does communication play in building a community? sustaining a community? For example, how do you think the invention of the telephone altered the way people communicated? How did the invention of radio and TV? How has each affected the way people define their community? How is the Internet altering communication today? How does it affect the way people define their community today?

Throughout *Choosing to Participate*, you will encounter words that you know but may have difficulty explaining. Instead of relying only on a dictionary to define those words, develop your own working definitions. The following is an example of a working definition that builds to encompass more and more information. It is one to which you will want to add your own ideas.

Community:
• a group of people with a shared goal
• a group of people who live near one another
• a group that is part of one's universe of obligation

Based on your working definition of a community, list the communities to which you belong. What do you have in common with other members of these communities? What responsibilities or obligations does membership involve? What are the privileges of membership? What does it take to get along in a group?

Marian Wright Edelman writes that "the segregated and hostile outside world. . . told us we weren't important." How was that message conveyed? How did it shape her identity–her sense of who she was and what she might become? In what ways did her parents and other adults try to counter that judgment? How did those efforts affect the way Edelman saw herself? her view of the world?

Writer Julius Lester grew up in Nashville, Tennessee, in the 1940s and 1950s. He describes segregation as "a deathly spiritual violence, not only in its many restrictions on where we could live, eat, go to school, and go after dark. There was also the constant threat of physical death if you looked at a white man in what he considered the wrong way or if he didn't like your attitude."[6] Why does Lester compare segregation to violence? How are the two connected?

Margot Stern Strom, the executive director of Facing History and Ourselves, grew up in Memphis, Tennessee, in the late 1940s and 1950s. She recalls:

> I grew up in a city where "colored" water fountains did not spout
> brightly colored water as a child might expect, but stood as
> symbols of the dogmas of racism. . . . I grew up in a city where

"colored day" at the zoo was Thursday, the only day African American children could visit, and where their library housed discarded books from our library. . . . I grew up knowing that there would always be empty seats on the bus for young white girls while those with a darker skin color would be crowded into the back. . . . In school my teachers carefully avoided any mention of "colored water fountains," seating arrangements on city buses, and other manifestations of Jim Crow. There was a powerful silence about race and racism.[7]

What is Margot Stern Strom suggesting about the way she and other white children learned about the privileges of being white in a segregated society? What does her account suggest about the difficulties in changing the attitudes, values, and beliefs that supported segregation?

 Watch this video:
www.facinghistory.org/video/congressman-john-lewis-talks-about-bringing-

[1] Irving Dillard, *The Spirit of Liberty: Papers and Addresses of Learned Hand* (New York: Alfred A. Knopf, 1963), 190.

[2] Lerone Bennett, Jr., *Before the Mayflower: A History of Black America* (Chicago: Johnson Publishing Company, 1982), 256.

[3] Marian Wright Edelman, *The Measure of Our Success: A Letter to My Children and Yours* (Boston: Beacon Press, 1992), 3–9, 33.

[4] Suzanne Goldsmith, *A City Year: On the Streets and in the Neighborhoods with Twelve Young Community Service Volunteers* (New York: The New Press, 1993), 277.

[5] Helen Fein, *Accounting for Genocide* (London: The Free Press), 33.

[6] Julius Lester, *Falling Pieces of the Broken Sky* (New York: Little, Brown and Company, 1990), 71.

[7] Margot Stern Strom, "A Work in Progress," as quoted in *Working to Make a Difference: The Personal and Pedagogical Stories of Holocaust Educators across the Globe*, edited by Samuel Totten (Lanham: Lexington Books, 2003), 69–70.

Ｈｏw much do you know about the people you go to school with?
Where have they come from? What challenges have they overcome?
What have they achieved? What stories do they have to tell? What do
they know about you?

Arn Chorn Pond in Cambodia, 2002.

Image courtesy of the Emmy nominated documentary film *The Flute Player*, 2003 © Over The Moon Productions, Inc.

Arn Chorn had a terrible story to tell but could not tell it. When Arn arrived in the United States he was 15 years old and already the survivor of the Cambodian Genocide. Arn's childhood was interrupted when the Khmer Rouge, a fanatical communist movement led by Pol Pot, overthrew the government of Cambodia and systematically tore apart the country–targeting minorities, artists, educated people, and the middle class for re-education and death. The population of the cities was forcibly relocated to communal farms where soldiers of the government brutally enforced the new order. Ordinary Cambodians starved while others were worked to death. Many people from outside of Cambodia offered aide, but the Khmer Rouge turned away their offers.

Arn remembers that at the age of nine he was forcibly separated from his own family and taken to a Khmer Rouge detention center. At the camp, a master musician taught Arn how to play the traditional wood Cambodian flute. After his teacher was killed, Arn was able to save his own life by performing propaganda songs for the soldiers. Arn remembers:

> They let me play music for them, and I knew music could save
> my life, because the Khmer Rouge wanted to kill me also. . .
> [b]ecause I looked white, my fingers were long, and they
> thought I was from a rich family, so they wanted to kill me, but

they couldn't do that because I was out to play music for them, and I was good at it.[1]

As a young boy, Arn learned the rules of survival. After watching a friend killed for crying, Arn learned to close down his own emotions. He explains, "I literally learned how to feel nothing. I made myself numb. I made myself not feel anything. I shut myself completely."[2]

Before long, he was forced into action as a child soldier, defending the very regime that ripped him from his own family. Arn was one of thousands of young people used by the Khmer Rouge to fight in their war against Vietnam. He remembers:

> I wanted to escape from the Khmer Rouge, but I knew they would kill me if I tried. I thought my life couldn't get any worse, but when the Vietnamese invaded Cambodia in 1979, the Khmer Rouge gave me an AK-47 and put me on the frontlines of battle. I was 14 years old. All the boys around me were getting their heads blown off. . . and I just couldn't take it anymore. So I ran away from the Vietnamese, and I ran away from the Khmer Rouge. I ran off by myself into the jungle. I had no food to eat, I eat barks, I follow the monkey. Whatever they eat, I eat. I was very lonely. After a few months, I found my way across the border to Thailand.[3]

By luck and chance, Arn made his way to a refugee camp along the Thai border. There he met Peter Pond, a Unitarian-Universalist minister from New Hampshire. Pond adopted Arn and several other Cambodian children and brought them to their new home in the United States.

Arn's home in rural New Hampshire was nothing like Cambodia. Not only was Arn among the first Cambodian refugees to come to the United States, but he and his brothers were the only non-white children at White Mountain Regional High School. Going to school was a difficult adjustment. Before the Khmer Rouge came to power Arn had attended a Buddhist school taught by monks. White Mountain High School was completely different. He remembers the swarm of students leaving classes "like bees." They would pass in the hall, some saying nothing or just staring at him. Others tried to reach out and make friends with him, but Arn couldn't understand them.

He didn't speak English. In interviews for *Choosing to Participate*, Arn, his adopted mother, one of his school teachers, a classmate, and his principal remember the difficult transition to the school:

> SHIRLEY POND: (Arn's adoptive mother):. . . The New Hampshire kids weren't sure of them. . . . They might know elaborate kung-fu kinds of things, and so they didn't dare push too much. But one of them would say, "Hello, fried rice," you know smart remarks. . . .

> ARN CHORN POND: American kids love to do that and [are] very good, very good in doing that, in making fun of you, making face[s].

> PAT KELLY (Arn's principal): Some of the other kids sometimes would get them to do things that they weren't supposed to. . . teenagers picking on other teenagers. . . . If there were racial slurs. . . I'm sure they faced that. . . . We had just come out of the Vietnam time period. . . . There were still prejudices involved with Asian students.

> ARN CHORN POND: Before I became like a soccer star. . . they were making fun of me. . . . You know they come put their arms, their hand on my head. . . they go bang, bang, bang and say "Arn, Arn, Arn". . . and they laugh.

> SUZANNE SCHOTT (Arn's English teacher): . . . I heard on more than one occasion. . . that phrase "gook," which I was appalled at. . . .

> JEFF WOODBURN (one of Arn's classmates): . . . You know there may have been slurs. . . . People just didn't know any better. . . .

> ARN CHORN POND: It hurts. It's very hurtful for me and I felt like nobody was on my side or something, and that's enough. . . to get me crazy.[4]

One place where Arn fit in was on the soccer field. Arn became a soccer star, leading his school's team to the state championship. In fact, he was so good that he became a target for people on the other teams. Jeff Woodburn explains, "He was just a lot better than most of us and other teams didn't like that. . . I'm sure there were slurs, I'm sure he was knocked down."

Arn remembers, "In Cambodia, in the jungle if somebody d[id] that to me, I [would] shoot them, that's what the Khmer Rouge taught me. . . . I was really happy and proud of myself that even though they hit me. . . I didn't hit them back."[5]

Despite his on-the-field successes, Arn still struggled in class. He day-dreamed about life in Cambodia, [as a soldier] and of fighting and smelling blood. Unable to speak English, Arn could not tell others about the pressure that he felt. Arn recalls, "Some of the kids. . . really want[ed] to reach out to me, but the big problem was the language."[7]

Pat Garvin, an ESL teacher, kept pushing Arn. She believed that Arn and his brothers "needed to speak in order to come alive again." She explained, "There is more than just learning the language going on. This is a chance for them to pull themselves back together, pull all these stories and threads of their life back into a whole person."[8]

Arn's father, Peter Pond, pushed Arn as well. He encouraged Arn to share his story with others, not only for himself, but as a way of educating people about Cambodia. Arn's first public speech was in front of 10,000 people at St. John the Divine Cathedral in New York. Arn recalls, "That [speech] was really a kind of. . . turning point for me. . . . I c[ould] speak now and people liked what I said. . . . You c[ould] hear a pin drop there. And I cried. . .because, I felt like you had power. . . . This. . . is very different from having power with guns. I feel power just standing there and talk[ing] for the first time. . . ."[9]

He explains:

> I was able to speak out about my life. I feel better. I learn how to cry in public. . . . [For] my first speech. . . I memorized the words by heart. Just, my name is Arn, my family [was] killed in Cambodia, a few words. And then there's this little girl [with] blond hair, coming and hugged me very tight. She's just about 10, about my age when I was in Cambodia, and she look[s] at me in the eyes. She said, "You know Arn, I'm sorry for what happened to you. I don't wish anything [like that to] happen to anybody, to any children like that." And she gave me a dollar,

said "Here, one dollar, maybe you can help other children." I never forgot that, because that made me feel very good. . . I think to myself that if I speak about it, there's somebody who cares. It's all in my head. Now it's true. Now, everywhere I go, [I get even] stronger. I get standing ovations.[10]

As Arn began to speak more, he began to see himself differently: "I got it, that I need to involve young American kids to know about what I went through and they need to know about me, I need to know about them, we all didn't know about each other."[11]

Jeff Woodburn, Arn's former classmate, believes that Arn had a tremendous impact on his community. Jeff explains, "What I would tell Arn if he was here today would be how much of an influence he's had on so many people in this area. . . . He's opened up the minds of a lot of people from my generation who. . . are [now]. . . more accepting of people who are different from us."

Today, Arn tells his audiences that everyone has a story to tell, including "the people next to you, [who] you didn't even notice because you [were] too busy." Arn explains that in school, "I was sitting next to a white boy. . . they didn't notice. . . that I have a story to share. I didn't know that he has a story to share either, so we didn't share."[13]

Inspired by the responses he received when he spoke, Arn, with the help of activist Judith Thompson, founded the group Children of War for children who were involved in war to come together, tell their stories, and speak out against injustice. His work didn't stop there. Today, the former child soldier is dedicated to promoting peace and human rights. Arn seeks out ways to express the power of nonviolence to anybody who will listen, from diplomats to gang members to prisoners. In the late 1990s, Arn returned to Cambodia to see how he could help the country continue to repair from the scars left by the Khmer Rouge.

When he returns to the United States, Arn continues to speak about all that he has seen–from his experiences in Cambodia to his struggles as a refugee in New Hampshire to his role as a human rights activist who has traveled the world. Arn reminds young people that "you have a lot of stuff that you want to share. . . . [T]he resources you have here, the love you have here, the freedom you have here, that's a good thing and don't take it for granted. . .a person will touch you and you will help millions. That's what we should do in our life, so go like angels."[14]

After hearing him speak, a high school student from Boston described the power of Arn's message:

> He told us about the suffering he went through and we really felt that we were right there with him. . .I've never heard any-thing in my whole life like this. . . . [Y]ou really wanted to sit there and hug him and cry. He wasn't a stranger any more after you heard what he had to say. . . . He said my eyes may be dif-ferent, my nose may be different, my mouth may be different, but the heart is the same, the soul is the same, and the feeling is the same. And, he made the point clearly that we are still one people.[15]

CONNECTIONS

How did Arn's classmates respond to him? Why do you think they respond-ed the way they did?

If you were one of Arn's classmates, what could you have done to help him make his way in his new school? Have you seen people ostracized in your school? How have people tried to prevent this from happening?

The teachers at White Mountain Regional High School struggled to find the best way to welcome Arn and his brothers. What does your school do to welcome new students?

Arn came to New Hampshire as an immigrant and a refugee. Are there im-migrants and refugees in your class? Where are they from? What stories do they have to tell? What might you learn from hearing about their experi-ences of moving to a new country? Who helps them learn about their new community?

Arn explains that in school, "I was sitting next to a boy. . . They didn't no-tice. . . that I have a story to share. I didn't know that he has a story to share either, so we didn't share." How much do you know about the people you go to school with? Are there some kids who you do not know much about?

Why do you think Arn believes that it is important to know each other's stories? How does sharing stories help to create community?

Why did Arn's teacher think it was so important for him to learn to share his story? What power did Arn discover when he first spoke about his experiences?

Arn remembers that power of speaking is "very different from having power with guns." What do you think he means?

How was Arn able to turn his story of victimization into a force for change? What enabled him to reach out to others?

Arn has inspired a number of people—from students to former gang members to diplomats—to work for peace. Who are the people in your life who have inspired you to make a difference?

Several films featuring Arn Chorn Pond are available from the Facing History and Ourselves resource library including *The Flute Player*, a documentary film that aired on PBS, and *Arn Chorn: Cambodian Survivor*, a Facing History event in which he speaks to students. He is profiled in *Broken Places and Participating in Democracy: Choosing to Make a Difference*. Arn is also one of the five human rights activists featured on Facing History and Ourselves' *Be the Change: Upstanders for Human Rights* website (www.facinghistory.org/bethechange).

 Watch this video:
www.facinghistory.org/video/arn-chorn-pond-everyone-has-a-story

[1] Rachel Laskow, "The Power of Music," *Scholastic News,* http://teacher.scholastic.com/scholasticnews/indepth/flute/latest_news/index.asp?article=man (accessed on July 12, 2007).

[2] Ibid.

[3] Arn Chorn Pond, *The Flute Player*, VHS, by Jocelyn Glatzer (Boston: Over the Moon Productions, Inc., 2003), http://www.pbs.org/pov/utils/pressroom/2003/thefluteplayer/transcript.pdf (accessed on July 12, 2007).

[4] Arn Chorn Pond, Jeff Woodburn, Shirley Pond, Pat Kelly, and Suzanne Schott, Interview by Facing History and Ourselves, September 21, 2006.

[5] Jeff Woodburn, Interview by Facing History and Ourselves, October 18, 2006.

[6] Arn Chorn Pond, Interview by Facing History and Ourselves, September 21, 2006.

[7] Ibid.

[8] Pat Garvin, Interview by Facing History and Ourselves, October 21, 2006.

[9] Arn Chorn Pond, Interview by Facing History and Ourselves, May 9, 2006.

[10] Arn Chorn Pond, Interview by Facing History and Ourselves, May 9, 2006, www.facinghistory.org/Campus/BeTheChange.nsf/TeacherResources Transcriptions?OpenForm#arn (accessed on July 16, 2007).

[11] Arn Chorn Pond, Interview by Facing History and Ourselves, September 21, 2006.

[12] Jeff Woodburn, Interview by Facing History and Ourselves, July 16, 2007.

[13] Arn Chorn Pond, Interview by Facing History and Ourselves, September 21, 2006.

[14] Ibid.

[15] Arn Chorn Pond, *Participating in Democracy: Choosing to Make a Difference*, VHS (Brookline: Facing History and Ourselves, 1995).

Reading 3

In the 1950s, segregation and ideas about "race" shaped the way Americans in all parts of the nation saw one another as well as the way they saw themselves. As writer Jesús Colón discovered on a subway ride in New York City, those ideas also influenced the decisions people made about one another.

It was very late at night on the eve of Memorial Day. She came into the subway at the 34th Street Pennsylvania Station. I am still trying to remember how she managed to push herself in with a baby on her right arm, a valise in her left hand and two children, a boy and girl about three and five years old, trailing after her. She was a nice-looking white lady in her early twenties.

Jesús Colón, author of "Little Things Are Big."

The Jésus Colón Papers, Archives of the Puerto Rican Diaspora, Ce ntro de Estudios Puertorriqueños, Hunter College, CUNY.

At Nevins Street, Brooklyn, we saw her preparing to get off at the next station–Atlantic Avenue–which happened to be the place where I too had to get off. Just as it was a problem for her to get on, it was going to be a problem for her to get off the subway with two small children to be taken care of, a baby on her right arm, and a medium-sized valise in her left hand.

And there I was, also preparing to get off at Atlantic Avenue, with no bundles to take care of–not even the customary book under my arm, without which I feel that I am not completely dressed.

As the train was entering the Atlantic Avenue station, some

white man stood up from his seat and helped her out, placing the children on the long, deserted platform. There were only two adult persons on the long platform some time after midnight on the eve of last Memorial Day.

I could perceive the steep, long concrete stairs going down to the Long Island Railroad or into the street. Should I offer my help as the American white man did at the subway door, placing the two children outside the subway car? Should I take care of the girl and the boy, take them by their hands until they reached the end of the steep, long concrete stairs of the Atlantic Avenue station?

Courtesy is a characteristic of the Puerto Rican. And here I was–a Puerto Rican hours past midnight, a valise, two white children and a white lady with a baby on her arm [badly] needing somebody to help her, at least until she descended the long concrete stairs.

But how could I, a Negro* and a Puerto Rican, approach this white lady, who very likely might have preconceived prejudices about Negroes and everybody with foreign accents, in a deserted subway station very late at night?

What would she say? What would be the first reaction of this white American woman perhaps coming from a small town with a valise, two children and a baby on her right arm? Would she say: Yes, of course, you may help me. Or would she think that I was just trying to get too familiar? Or would she think worse than that perhaps? What would I do if she let out a scream as I went forward to offer my help?

Was I misjudging her? So many slanders are written every day in the daily press against the Negroes and Puerto Ricans. I hesitated for a long, long minute. The ancestral manners that the most illiterate Puerto Rican passes on from father to son were struggling inside me. Here was I, way past midnight, face to face with a situation that could very well explode into an out-

*The word Negro was commonly used in the early and middle years of this century to refer to an African American. Its use reflects the time period.

burst of prejudices and chauvinistic conditioning of the "divide and rule" policy of present-day society.

It was a long minute. I passed on by her as if I saw nothing. As if I was insensitive to her need. Like a rude animal walking on two legs, I just moved on, half running by the long subway platform, leaving the children and the valise and her with the baby on her arm. I took the steps of the long concrete stairs in twos until I reached the street above and the cold air slapped my warm face.

This is what racism and prejudice and chauvinism and official artificial divisions can do to people and to a nation!

Perhaps the lady was not prejudiced after all. Or not prejudiced enough to scream at the coming of a Negro toward her in a solitary subway station a few hours past midnight.

If you were not that prejudiced, I failed you, dear lady. I know that there is a chance in a million that you will read these lines. I am willing to take the millionth chance. If you were not that prejudiced, I failed you, lady. I failed you, children. I failed myself to myself.

I buried my courtesy early on Memorial Day morning. But here is a promise that I make to myself here and now; if I am ever faced with an occasion like that again, I am going to offer my help regardless of how the offer is going to be received.

Then I will have my courtesy with me again.[1]

CONNECTIONS

Create an identity chart for Jesús Colón like the one below. It contains words individuals call themselves as well as the labels society gives them. What words does Colón use to describe himself? What words might others use to describe him? Include both on the diagram.

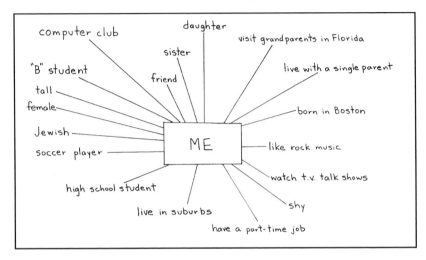

What dilemma does the narrator face? What risks does he perceive if he tries to help the woman? Would the dilemma have been different if the woman had been in danger? if the incident had taken place during the day?

Jesús Colón describes labels that others have placed on him. What labels does he place on the groups to which he belongs? on other groups? How did those labels shape the way he perceived his choices? the decision he made? Why does he have regrets? Did he make the right choice? Would your answer be different if he were a white American? Who is the victim in this story–Colón, the woman, or the larger society?

Political scientist Benjamin Barber defines *civility* as "a work of the imagination, for it is through the imagination that we render others sufficiently like ourselves that we view them as worthy of tolerance and respect, if not always affection."[2] What does *courtesy* mean? How are courtesy and civility related? Colón writes that he "buried his courtesy" that morning. What does he mean? What is the significance of that loss?

Create a different ending to Colón's story. What do you think Colón might have done? How do you think the woman might have responded to the action you have imagined for Colón? Describe the effect of that action on Colón.

 Watch this video:
www.facinghistory.org/video/little-things-are-big

[1] Jesús Colón, *A Puerto Rican in New York and Other Sketches* (New York: International Publishers, 1982), 115–17.
[2] Benjamin Barber, "America Skips School: Why We Talk So Much about Education and Do So Little," *Harper's Magazine* v287 (November 1993).

As the capital of the United States and home of the federal government, Washington, DC and all that happens there has a particular symbolic value. Throughout the twentieth and twenty-first centuries, activists have used the city's monuments and public spaces as a backdrop to highlight the importance of their cause. Possibly no location has become as loaded with symbolism as the Lincoln Memorial.

Marian Anderson performing for an estimated crowd of 75,000 on the steps of the Lincoln Memorial, 1939

Courtesy of Getty Images

In 1939 world famous black opera singer Marian Anderson planned to perform in Washington, DC as part of her American tour. Anderson was described as having an "imposing majesty" and possessed a "voice that even in speech still enthralled her listeners."[1] Organizers of the event, including faculty from the music department at the historically black Howard University, knew that the only theater in the city large enough to hold the expected audience would be Constitution Hall.

Three years earlier, Anderson was the first black artist to perform at the White House when she sang at the request of the first lady, Eleanor Roosevelt. But in 1939 Washington, DC was simultaneously segregated and integrated, both by law and by custom. The laws in Washington that mandated segregation in public schools and recreation facilities did not apply to public libraries or public transportation.[2] And even though blacks were customarily expected to sit in separate sections in white theaters, this custom was often abandoned and seating was mixed.[3] However, this was never the case in Constitution Hall, which was, and still is, owned by the Daughters of the American Revolution (DAR)—a genealogical women's organization whose members can trace their ancestors back to the patriots of the American Revolution.[4] Whereas many theaters had segregated seating for blacks and whites, the DAR adopted an uncommonly rigid policy that prevented black artists from performing at Constitution Hall. When the organizers of Marian Anderson's concert approached DAR president Mrs. Henry M. Robert, Jr. directly, she bluntly stated that no Negro artist would be permitted to appear [there].[5]

Though Anderson herself rarely spoke out about civil rights, her concert organizers and other civil rights leaders, including Howard University Treasurer V. D. Johnston and NAACP chairman Walter White, were vocal in their outrage on her behalf. In response, White, a personal friend of Mrs. Roosevelt, who was herself a DAR member, encouraged her to take a stand. Roosevelt considered how to respond.

Civil rights issues had become increasingly important to Mrs. Roosevelt. Just a few years before, she had attended a civil rights meeting in Birmingham, Alabama. When police insisted on separating blacks and whites, Roosevelt, who had been sitting on the black side of the aisle, moved her chair to the middle of the room in a symbolic act of protest. At the same time, Roosevelt was fully aware that as the first lady any action she took would soon become national news. Her husband, Franklin Delano Roosevelt, had to handle civil rights issues delicately during his presidency. Many of Congress's key committees were run by die-hard segregationists who resisted what they viewed as federal interference in their way of life. While Mrs. Roosevelt debated her response, the story of the DAR's refusal to allow Anderson to perform at Constitution Hall had begun to receive attention in the press. After strategizing with NAACP officials, black clergy, and the faculty and staff of Howard University, and United States Interior Secretary Harold Ickes, Roosevelt resigned her membership in the DAR. In her letter of resignation, Roosevelt explained her actions:

> I am in complete disagreement with the attitude taken in refusing Constitution Hall to a great artist. You have set an example which seems to me unfortunate. And I feel obliged to send in to you my resignation. You had an opportunity to lead in an enlightened way and it seems to me that your organization has failed.[6]

The next day, in her syndicated daily newspaper column, "My Day," Roosevelt explained that she usually believed in working within organizations to change their policies, even if it required a painfully long process. However, in this case, she felt that the DAR had left her no choice: "They have taken an action that was widely talked of in the press. To remain as a member implies approval of that action, and therefore I am resigning..." .[7] The same day that this column appeared, Anderson stated:

> I am not surprised at Mrs. Roosevelt's actions . . . because she seems to me to be one who really comprehends the true meaning of democracy. I am shocked beyond words to be barred from the capital of my own country after having appeared almost in every other capital in the world.[8]

Roosevelt's resignation and subsequent column made the DAR's racist actions a national sensation. While she was not the first to resign, her bold stand drew widespread attention to the DAR's segregationist policy, and newspapers around the country picked up the story. One *New York Times* editorial in particular captured the public's outrage:

> . . . Those who love music and are unable to perceive any relationship between music on the one hand and political, economic or social issues on the other will regret, as Mrs. Eleanor Roosevelt does, that Washington may be deprived of the pleasure of hearing this artist.
>
> If Miss Anderson's inability to find a suitable hall in the national capital for her April concert is due to social or racial snobbery, all that can be said is that such an attitude is inconsistent with the best American traditions, including those which were born in the fires of the American Revolution. It is hard to believe that any patriotic organization in this country would approve of discrimination against so gifted an artist and so fine a person as Miss Anderson. In fact, no organization could do so and still merit the adjective patriotic.
>
> We hope there has been some mistake. If there has not been, it is not Miss Anderson who has suffered most. She has, as before, the esteem and admiration of all those who love a golden voice and cherish American ideals.[9]

After Roosevelt's resignation, *The New York Times* published the results of a national survey about her actions:

> The vote for the country at large is:
>
> Approve of Mrs. Roosevelt's action in resigning. 67%
>
> Disapprove 33%
>
> Southerners dissented by an average vote of 57 per cent, but even some of the dissenters declared they had no objection to Marian Anderson's singing as a paid performer. It was Mrs. Roosevelt's "making a fuss about it" that they disliked.
>
> A majority of Democrats in Mrs. Roosevelt's own party approve of what she did, however, and it is interesting to note that most Republicans do likewise:
>
> Approve–Democrats, 68 per cent; Republicans, 63 per cent.
>
> Disapprove–Democrats, 32 per cent; Republicans, 37 per cent.[10]

Mrs. Roosevelt and others were still not satisfied. Despite the public outcry against the DAR's policy prohibiting black artists from appearing at Constitution Hall, Anderson, who had given concerts all over the world, still had no place to perform in the capital of her own country. White, Mrs. Roosevelt, Anderson's manager Sol Hurok, and Secretary of the Interior Harold L. Ickes came up with a bold plan that met with President Roosevelt's wholehearted approval. They arranged for Anderson to perform as planned in Washington, DC on Easter Sunday, April 9, 1939. Defying the culture of segregation, they organized an open air concert–open to all people–on the steps of the Lincoln Memorial. As reported in a *New York Times* article,

> [A]n enthusiastic crowd estimated at 75,000, including many government officials, stood at the foot of Lincoln Memorial today and heard Marian Anderson, Negro contralto, give a concert and tendered her an unusual ovation. Permission to sing in Constitution Hall had been refused Miss Anderson by the Daughters of the American Revolution.
>
> The audience, about half composed of Negroes, was gathered in a semi-circle at the foot of the great marble monument to

the man who emancipated the Negroes. It stretched half-way around the long reflecting pool. Miss Anderson was applauded heartily after each of her numbers and was forced to give an encore.

When the concert was finished the crowd, in attempting to congratulate Miss Anderson, threatened to mob her and police had to rush her back inside the Memorial where the heroic statue of Lincoln towers.. . .

Secretary Ickes, who granted Miss Anderson permission to sing at this site, sat on her right on the monument's plaza, just above the specially arranged platform from which Miss Anderson sang into six microphones that carried the sound of her voice for blocks and over radio channels to millions throughout the country. . . .

Miss Anderson wore a tan fur coat with a bright orange and yellow scarf about her throat. She was bareheaded. Her mother was present.

In introducing Miss Anderson, Mr. Ickes referred to the Washington Monument at one end of the reflecting pool and to the Lincoln Memorial and in an implied rebuke to the D.A.R. remarked that "in our own time too many pay mere lip service to these twin planets in our democratic heaven."

"In this great auditorium under the sky all of us are free," the Secretary asserted. "When God gave us this wonderful outdoors and the sun, the moon and the stars, He made no distinction of race, or creed, or color."

In a few brief remarks at the end of her concert Miss Anderson said: "I am so overwhelmed, I just can't talk. I can't tell you what you have done for me today. I thank you from the bottom of my heart again and again."[11]

The massive crowd extended from the Lincoln Memorial to the Washington Monument while all across the country radios turned to a national broadcast of the performance.[12] Reflecting on the concert in her autobiography, Anderson wrote, "All I knew then was the overwhelming impact of that vast multitude. . . . I had a feeling that a great wave of good will poured out from these people."[13]

Three months after the concert on July 2, 1939 in Richmond, VA, the former capital of the Confederacy, Eleanor Roosevelt presented Marian Anderson with the Spingarn Medal, the NAACP's highest honor. The concert continues to echo through the country's history. Two decades later, Martin Luther King, Jr. gave his famous "I Have a Dream" speech from those very steps, concluding his sermon with the first verse of "America" ("My Country, 'Tis of Thee")–the same song Marian Anderson used to open her program in 1939.[14] And nearly half a century later, a record two million people crowded in front of the Lincoln Memorial to witness the inauguration of President Barack Obama, the first African American president of the United States. At the inauguration, Aretha Franklin sang "America," bringing to mind Marian Anderson's historic concert 70 years earlier. Though Mrs. Roosevelt did not attend the concert,[15] her response was the driving force behind both Anderson's concert at the Lincoln Memorial in 1939 and the subsequently strengthened association of the Lincoln Memorial with the civil rights movement.

CONNECTIONS

Why do you think many scholars view these events in 1939 as a turning point in civil rights history?

How important was Mrs. Roosevelt's involvement in this story? How did she explain her decision to resign from the DAR? What do you think of her reasons?

Roosevelt explained that she usually preferred to work for change from within an organization. However, in this case she resigned. What are the advantages and disadvantages of each approach?

How did the setting of the Lincoln Memorial increase the impact of Anderson's concert? Under what circumstances do certain events–such as Anderson's concert–take on a symbolic meaning?

Like much of the country in 1939, Washington, DC mandated the segregation of some facilities but not others. What is the history of integration in your community? Have laws and customs ever kept groups of people apart where you live?

Often stories of social change highlight the role of only one or two leaders. After the DAR refused to allow Anderson to perform at Constitution Hall, Anderson could have cut Washington out of her American tour. Instead, the efforts of many individuals helped make Anderson's Easter Sunday concert at the Lincoln Memorial a reality. Name some of the different ways in which people might support such an event.

The DAR later apologized to Anderson and invited her to perform at Constitution Hall for a benefit concert in 1942. They reversed their whites-only policy in 1952; and when the US Post Office issued a commemorative stamp bearing Anderson's image in 2005, the ceremony celebrating the occasion was held at Constitution Hall. How important are such gestures for making amends?

Watch this video:
http://www.youtube.com/watch?v=wQnzb0Jj074.

---

[1] Joseph P. Lash, *Eleanor and Franklin: The Story of Their Relationship, Based on Eleanor Roosevelt's Private Papers* (New York: W. W. Norton & Company, 1971), 525.

[2] Marya Annette McQuirter, "African Americans in Washington, DC: 1800–1975," *Washington: Cultural Tourism* DC (2003), http://www.culturaltourismdc.org/information3949/information_show.htm?doc_id=208984 (accessed May 18, 2009).

[3] Allan, Keiler, *Marian Anderson: A Singer's Journey* (Champaign, IL: University of Illinois Press, 2002), 188–89; 191.

[4] "Who We Are," DAR *National Society* (2005), http://www.dar.org/natsociety/whoweare.cfm (accessed on May 18, 2009).

[5] Lash, *Eleanor and Franklin*, 525.

[6] "Eleanor Roosevelt's Letter of Resignation," Franklin D. Roosevelt Presidential Library and Museum, http://www.fdrlibrary.marist.edu/tmirhfee.html (accessed March 4, 2009).

[7] Eleanor Roosevelt, *My Day*, February 27, 1939.

[8] "Mrs. Roosevelt Indicates She Has Resigned From D.A.R. Over Refusal of Hall to Negro," *The New York Times*, February 27, 1939.

[9] "Marian Anderson," *The New York Times*, March 1, 1939; ProQuest Historical Newspapers, The New York Times, 17

[10] "Mrs. Roosevelt Approved," *The New York Times*; March 19, 1939; ProQuest Historical Newspapers, The New York Times, 58.

[11] "Throng Honors Marian Anderson In Concert at Lincoln Memorial" *The New York Times*. April 10, 1939; ProQuest Historical Newspapers, *The New York Times*, 15.

[12] *The Washington Post*, April 10, 1939

[13] Anderson, Marian, *My Lord, What a Morning: An Autobiography* (Champaign, IL: University of Illinois Press, 2002), 191.

[14] Alex Ross, "Voice of the Century: Celebrating Marian Anderson," *The New Yorker*, April 13, 2009, 78, 79.

[15] Lash, *Eleanor and Franklin*, 527. Other documents related to this event can be found at the National Archives and Records Administration's website, http://www.archives.gov/exhibits/american_originals/elenor.html (accessed January 16, 2009).

Reading 5

Like Jesús Colón in the reading "Little Things are Big," many of us have been in situations where we wanted to help people in need but did not act. When asked why they didn't act, people often say that they were not sure what to do and did not know how to make a difference. Such feelings are often magnified when the injustice is thousands of miles away. In his article "Save the Darfur Puppy," *New York Times* columnist Nicholas D. Kristof summarizes the challenges of motivating people to take action during a humanitarian crisis:

> Finally, we're beginning to understand what it would take to galvanize President Bush, other leaders and the American public to respond to the genocide in Sudan: a suffering puppy with big eyes and floppy ears.
>
> That's the implication of a series of studies by psychologists trying to understand why people–good, conscientious people–aren't moved by genocide or famines. Time and again, we've seen that the human conscience just isn't pricked by mass suffering, while an individual child (or puppy) in distress causes our hearts to flutter.
>
> In one experiment, psychologists asked ordinary citizens to contribute $5 to alleviate hunger abroad. In one version, the money would go to a particular girl, Rokia, a 7-year-old in Mali; in another, to 21 million hungry Africans; in a third, to Rokia–but she was presented as a victim of a larger tapestry of global hunger.
>
> Not surprisingly, people were less likely to give to anonymous millions than to Rokia. But they were also less willing to give in the third scenario, in which Rokia's suffering was presented as part of a broader pattern.
>
> Evidence is overwhelming that humans respond to the suffering of individuals rather than groups . . . .
>
> Even the right animal evokes a similar sympathy. A dog stranded on a ship aroused so much pity that $48,000 in pri-

vate money was spent trying to rescue it–and that was before the Coast Guard stepped in. And after I began visiting Darfur in 2004, I was flummoxed by the public's passion to save a red-tailed hawk, Pale Male, that had been evicted from his nest on Fifth Avenue in New York City. A single homeless hawk aroused more indignation than two million homeless Sudanese.

Advocates for the poor often note that 30,000 children die daily of the consequences of poverty–presuming that this number will shock people into action. But the opposite is true: the more victims, the less compassion.

In one experiment, people in one group could donate to a $300,000 fund for medical treatments that would save the life of one child–or, in another group, the lives of eight children. People donated more than twice as much money to help save one child as to help save eight.

Likewise, remember how people were asked to save Rokia from starvation? A follow-up allowed students to donate to Rokia or to a hungry boy named Moussa. Both Rokia and Moussa attracted donations in the same proportions. Then another group was asked to donate to Rokia and Moussa together. But donors felt less good about supporting two children, and contributions dropped off.

"Our capacity to feel is limited," Paul Slovic of the University of Oregon writes in a new journal article, "Psychic Numbing and Genocide," which discusses these experiments. Professor Slovic argues that we cannot depend on the innate morality even of good people. Instead, he believes, we need to develop legal or political mechanisms to force our hands to confront genocide.

One experiment underscored the limits of rationality. People prepared to donate to the needy were first asked either to talk about babies (to prime the emotions) or to perform math calculations (to prime their rational side). Those who did math donated less.

So maybe what we need isn't better laws but more troubled consciences—pricked, perhaps, by a Darfur puppy with big eyes and floppy ears. . . .[1]

What does it take for people to get involved? In studies of rescuers during genocide, Ervin Staub states,

> Goodness, like evil, often begins in small steps. Heroes evolve; they aren't born. Very often the rescuers make only a small commitment at the start—to hide someone for a day or two. But once they had taken that step, they began to see themselves differently, as someone who helps. What starts as mere willingness becomes intense involvement.[2]

Nicholas Winton was a 29-year-old stockbroker living comfortably in his home in Hempstead, England when the Nazis marched into Czechoslovakia. As the Nazis annexed the *Sudetenland**, thousands of refugees fled for safety. Unlike the subjects in the stories and studies Kristof cites, Winton took action. The website for "Nicholas Winton: The Power of Good"—a 2002 Emmy Award—winning documentary about Winton's story—describes what happened next:

Nicholas Winton holding one of the 669 children he rescued, 1939

> In December 1938, Nicholas Winton, a 29-year-old London stockbroker, was about to leave for a skiing holiday in Switzerland, when he received a phone call from his friend Martin Blake asking him to cancel his holiday and immediately come to Prague: *"I have a most interesting assignment and I need your help. Don't bother bringing your skis."* When Winton arrived, he was asked to help in the camps, in which thousands of refugees were living in appalling conditions.

In October 1938, after the ill-fated Munich Agreement between Germany and the Western European powers, the Nazis annexed a large part of western Czechoslovakia, the *Sudetenland*. Winton was convinced that the German occupation of the rest of the country would soon follow . . . .

"I found out that the children of refugees and other groups of people who were enemies of Hitler weren't being looked after. I decided to try to get permits to Britain for them. I found out that the conditions which were laid down for bringing in a child were chiefly that you had a family that was willing and able to look after the child, and £50, which was quite a large sum of money in those days, that was to be deposited at the Home Office."* The situation was heartbreaking . . . . The parents desperately wanted at least to get their children to safety when they couldn't manage to get visas for the whole family. . . ."

In terms of his mission, Winton was not thinking in small numbers, but of thousands of children. He was ready to start a mass evacuation.

"Everybody in Prague said, 'Look, there is no organization in Prague to deal with refugee children, nobody will let the children go on their own, but if you want to have a go, have a go.' And I think there is nothing that can't be done if it is fundamentally reasonable."

. . . Nicholas Winton set up his own rescue operation. At first, Winton's office was a dining room table at his hotel in Wenceslas Square in Prague. . . . Soon, an office was set up. . . . Thousands of parents heard about this unique endeavor and hundreds of them lined up in front of the new office . . . .

Great Britain promised to accept children under the age of 18 as long as he found homes and guarantors who could deposit

---

* Sudentenland refers to the land incorporated into the western regions of Czechoslovakia. These regions were inhabited predominantly by ethnic Germans. In 1938, Munich conference participants gave in to Hitler and transferred Sudentenland to Germany—a precursor to Hitler's conquest of all of Czechoslovakia. Sudetenland was restored to Czechosolovakia after World War II, and most German inhabitants were kicked out.

£50 for each child to pay for their return home . . . .

Winton returned to London . . . . He worked at his regular job on the Stock Exchange by day, and then devoted late afternoons and evenings to his rescue efforts, often working far into the night. He made up an organization, calling it "The British Committee for Refugees from Czechoslovakia, Children's Section." The committee consisted of himself, his mother, his secretary and a few volunteers.

Winton had to find funds to use for repatriation costs, and a foster home for each child. He also had to raise money to pay for the transports when the children's parents could not cover the costs. . . . Finding sponsors was only one of the endless problems in obtaining the necessary documents from German and British authorities.

"Officials at the Home Office worked very slowly with the entry visas. We went to them urgently asking for permits, only to be told languidly, 'Why rush, old boy? Nothing will happen in Europe.' This was a few months before the war broke out. So we forged the Home Office entry permits."

On March 14, 1939, Winton had his first success: the first transport of children left Prague for Britain by airplane. Winton managed to organize seven more transports that departed from Prague's Wilson Railway Station. The groups then crossed the English Channel by boat and finally ended their journey at London's Liverpool Street station . . . .

The last trainload of children left on August 2, 1939, bringing the total of rescued children to 669 . . . .

On September 1, 1939 the biggest transport of children was to take place, but on that day Hitler invaded Poland, and all borders controlled by Germany were closed. This put an end to Winton's rescue efforts . . . .

"Within hours of the announcement, the train disappeared.

<hr>

" The sum of £50 at that time was equivalent to around $3,000 today.

None of the 250 children aboard was seen again. We had 250 families waiting at Liverpool Street that day in vain. If the train had been a day earlier, it would have come through. Not a single one of those children was heard of again, which is an awful feeling."

. . . After the war, Nicholas Winton didn't tell anyone, not even his wife Grete[,] about his wartime rescue efforts. In 1988, a half century later, Grete found a scrapbook from 1939 in their attic, with all the children's photos, a complete list of names, a few letters from parents of the children to Winton and other documents. She finally learned the whole story. . . .[3]

In 1988 on Esther Rantzen's BBC television program "That's Life," Winton was reunited with many of the children he rescued. The documentary "Nicholas Winton: The Power of Good" includes footage of the reunion. Despite the widespread public recognition for his humanitarian actions, Winton insists that he is not a hero. He explains, "I was never in any danger. I took on a big task, but did it from the safety of my home in Hampstead."[4]

CONNECTIONS

Have you ever been in a situation where you were aware of an injustice but did not take action? What stopped you from getting involved?

In "Save the Darfur Puppy," Kristof describes a series of studies about why people do not reach out to help victims of genocide or famine. What does the research suggest? Why do you think some people reach out to people in need while others remain bystanders?

What can we learn from Winton's story? How were his actions different from those of the research subjects Kristof describes? What do you think motivated Winton to get involved?

Why does Winton insist that he is not a hero? What point is he trying to make?

Copies of the film "Nicholas Winton: The Power of Good" are available for Facing History and Ourselves teachers from our Resource library.

The film "Reporter," which follows journalist Kristof as he researches and writes about human rights for *The New York Times,* is also available from the Facing History and Ourselves Resource library.

 Watch this video: Download a 6-minute preview of "The Power of Good" at: http://www.powerofgood.net/

[1] Nicholas D. Kristof, "Save the Darfur Puppy," *New York Times* (May 10, 2007), http://select.nytimes.com/2007/05/10/opinion/10kristof.html (accessed on June 12, 2009).

[2] Daniel Goldman, "Is Altruism Inherited?" *Baltimore Jewish Times* (April 12, 1985): 70.

[3] "The Story," *Nicholas Winton: The Power of Good* (2009), http://www.powerofgood.net/story.php (accessed July 12, 2009)

[4] Monica Porter, "Sir Nicholas Winton: A Reluctant Holocaust Hero," *The Jewish Community* Online (May 14, 2009), http://www.thejc.com/articles/sir-nicholas-winton-a-reluctant-holocaust-hero (accessed July 11, 2009).

In the early 1900s, "race" was the lens through which many Americans viewed the world. It was a lens that shaped ideas about who belonged and who did not. These were years when only a few people resisted Jim Crow laws. That resistance took many forms. Some worked quietly to change attitudes and values. Others openly expressed their outrage, while a few advocated violence.

During those years, Americans who opposed segregation concentrated on providing young African Americans with the skills necessary to openly challenge discrimination. They founded a variety of vocational schools, colleges, and universities open to young people of all races and ethnicities. In time, a number of lawyers trained at these institutions began to chip away at segregation in court. With the support of the National Association for the Advancement of Colored People (NAACP), they attacked Jim Crow laws—particularly laws that affected educational opportunities—case by case. They began with state-supported universities and then focused their attention on segregation in the nation's public schools. On May 17, 1954, in *Brown v. Board of Education*, the U.S. Supreme Court ruled unanimously in their favor. The justices decided that separate schools for black and white children were not and never could be equal.

Marian Wright Edelman (Reading 1) recalls, "My father and I waited anxiously for the *Brown v. Board of Education* decision in 1954. We talked about it and what it would mean for my future and for the future of millions of other black children. He died the week before Brown was decided. But I and other children lucky enough to have caring and courageous parents and other role models were able, in later years, to walk through the new and heavy doors that Brown slowly and painfully opened—doors that some are trying to close again today."[1]

The choices made by ordinary people—young and old, black and white—determined how quickly and easily those doors would open. In a few communities, doors opened with little debate. In others, even the possibility of limited integration aroused old hatreds and gave new life to old myths and misinformation about race.

In the fall of 1957, those who favored segregation and those who opposed it were riveted to their TV sets, as they watched a crisis unfold in Little Rock, Arkansas. Journalist David Halberstam described it as "the first all-out confrontation between the force of the law and the force of the mob, played out with television cameras whirring away in black and white for a nation that was by now largely wired."[2] After watching the confrontation on television, Doris Kearns Goodwin, then a high school student in New York, wrote a letter to President Dwight D. Eisenhower urging him to intervene. Goodwin recalls:

> Aside from the death of [actor] James Dean and the struggle to keep the Dodgers in Brooklyn, no public event had so fully engaged my private emotions. To challenge the president of the country, to berate angrily a governor I had never heard of from a place I did not know, was for me an immense expansion of political consciousness. It was a turning point or, at least, the start of a turning point.[3]

Yet as late as the summer of 1957, few people expected Little Rock to become the center of a crisis over integration. Hardly anyone there protested in 1955 when the school board announced a plan to integrate one high school beginning in the fall of 1957. And there was no outcry when school officials approved 17 African American students from over 200 applicants for enrollment at Central High, one of three all-white high schools in the city.

As fall neared, however, resistance to integration became more vocal in Little Rock and elsewhere. A number of African American students responded by withdrawing their applications. By the time school opened, only nine were prepared to attend Central High School–Minnijean Brown, Elizabeth Eckford, Ernest Green, Thelma Mothershed, Melba Pattillo, Gloria Ray, Terrence Roberts, Jefferson Thomas, and Carlotta Walls. Despite the talk on TV, over the radio, and in the newspapers, they did not believe that integration would lead to violence in Little Rock. Ernest Green recalls:

> There hadn't been any trouble expected, given the fact that there had been other schools in Arkansas that had been integrated–Fort Smith, Arkansas, and some others. The buses in Little Rock had been desegregated without any problem.

Arkansas National Guard troops blocking students trying to enter Little Rock Central High School, September 1957.

The library was integrated, the medical school, and the law school at the University had admitted some blacks. So there was an expectation that there would be minimal problems, but nothing major that would put Little Rock on the map. The first inclination that I had of it was the night before we were to go to school, the Labor Day Monday night. [Governor] Orval Faubus came on TV and indicated that he was calling out the [Arkansas] National Guard to prevent our entrance into Central because of what he thought were threats to our lives. He was doing it for our own "protection." Even at that time that was his line. He said that the troops would be out in front of the school and they would bar our entrance to Central–for our protection as well as for the protection and tranquility of the city.[4]

Tuesday morning, school officials asked the "Little Rock Nine" to stay home, while they sought guidance from U.S. District Judge Ronald N. Davies. He ordered integration to proceed as planned. The nine black students were told to report to Central High the next morning. Fearful for their safety, Daisy Bates, the president of the Arkansas NAACP, suggested that they come to school as a group. She asked white and black religious leaders to accompany them.

Fifteen-year-old Elizabeth Eckford knew nothing of the plan. In her haste, Daisy Bates forgot to get word to her. So early Wednesday morning, Eckford set off for school, alone.

When she reached Central High, she found herself surrounded by an angry crowd. As they screamed and threatened, she tried to enter the building only to be turned away by soldiers armed with bayonets. Unsure what to do and terrified by the mob, Eckford quickly headed for a bus stop even as the crowd continued to spit and scream, taunt and jeer. She later said of her ordeal, "I remember this tremendous feeling of being alone, and I didn't know how I was going to get out of there. I didn't know whether I would be injured. There was this deafening roar. I could hear individual voices, but I was not conscious of numbers. I was conscious of being alone."

A few minutes later, as a second black student, Terrence Roberts, approached the school, the soldiers formed a human fence to keep him out. Although the crowd taunted Roberts, it was Eckford who bore the brunt of their anger. As she sat on a bench with tears streaming down her face, Benjamin Fine of *The New York Times* tried to comfort her. Then a white woman, Grace Lorch, suddenly confronted the mob. Fine reported:

> "She's scared," Mrs. Lorch said. "She's just a little girl." She appealed to the men and women around her.
>
> "Why don't you calm down?" she asked. "I'm not here to fight with you. Six months from now you'll be ashamed at what you're doing."
>
> "Go home, you're just one of them," Mrs. Lorch was told.
>
> She escorted the Negro student to the other side of the street, but the crowd followed.
>
> "Won't somebody please call a taxi?" she pleaded. She was met with hoot calls and jeers.
>
> Finally, after being jostled by the crowd, she worked her way to the street corner, and the two boarded a bus.
>
> Seven other Negro students tried to get into the school. They came together, accompanied by four white ministers. Dunbar Ogden, president of the Greater Little Rock Ministerial

Association, acted as spokesman for the group.

"Sorry, we cannot admit Negro students," the officers of the militia told them.

The crowd began to disperse slowly. Many of the students who had waited outside the school building to see whether the Negroes would enter, started to go into school. They had said that if the Negroes went in, they would go out.[5]

For 17 days, the Arkansas National Guard kept the Little Rock Nine from entering Central High, but did nothing to disperse the crowd of angry whites that gathered outside the building. Perlesta Hollingsworth, an African American who lived near Central High, told a reporter many years later, "The shocking thing to me in 1957 was the number of whites who didn't participate in the aggression, who wouldn't do anything but look. Neighbors would express dismay, but wouldn't do anything, wouldn't speak out against it, would go ahead and close their doors to it."[6]

Marcia Webb was among those whites. She was a student at Central High at the time and a bystander the day the mob harassed Elizabeth Eckford. She was also a witness to the crowds that surrounded the school in the days that followed. As an adult, she reflected on the choices she made then:

The things that I thought about when I was in high school were.
. . the things that most kids did in the '50s. . . the football team.
. . dances. . . . I think it was a white person's world–probably a white man's world. Most of the blacks you had any contact with in 1957 were your household workers, sanitation department helpers, and that would be the only contact you would have. But I remember the picture in the newspaper of Elizabeth Eckford with the jeering white faces behind her. And at that moment I thought, Marcie, you were there and you never once thought about what was going on with Elizabeth Eckford. You were glad there weren't any violent demonstrations, you were glad no one was hurt physically. But then I realized what hurt can come from words, from silence even, from just being ignored. And when I think about it now I think about it with regret. I'm sorry to say now looking back that what was happening didn't have more significance and I didn't take more of an active role. But I was

interested in the things that most kids are.

On Friday, September 20, Judge Davies ruled that the state could not continue to block integration. Governor Faubus responded to the court order by withdrawing the Arkansas National Guard.

The following Monday, about one hundred Little Rock police officers placed wooden barricades around Central High as more than a thousand angry white men and women from Arkansas and surrounding states gathered in front of the building. To avoid the mob, the African American students entered the school through a side door. After learning the students were in the building, the crowd went on a rampage.

By midmorning, the mob had attacked both black and white journalists, broken windows and doors in the school, and come close to capturing the Little Rock Nine. The police had to smuggle them out of the school for their own safety. Melba Pattillo later said of that day:

> The first time, the first day I was able to enter Central High
> School, what I felt inside was stark raving fear—terrible,
> wrenching, awful fear. . . . There are no words for how I felt
> inside. I had known no pain like that because I did not know
> what I had done wrong. You see, when you're fifteen years old
> and someone's going to hit you or hurt you, you want to know
> what you did wrong. Although I knew the differences between
> black and white, I didn't know the penalties one paid for being
> black at that time.

The next day, President Dwight Eisenhower, outraged by the violence, ordered the 101st Airborne Division to Little Rock. On September 25, American soldiers not only dispersed the mob but also escorted the Little Rock Nine to school. This time, Melba Pattillo recalls, "I went in not through the side doors, but up the front stairs, and there was a feeling of pride and hope that yes, this is the United States; yes, there is a reason I salute the flag; and it's going to be okay."

Eisenhower's decision surprised many Americans. He did not favor integration. Born in 1890, he grew up in a segregated society and served for more than 30 years in a segregated army. Not long after the *Brown* decision, he remarked, "You can't change people's hearts merely by laws." He also told reporters that he could not imagine a situation in which he would use federal troops to enforce integration. Yet after watching events in Little Rock, he ordered federal troops to the city to enforce the law. He told the American people: "Our personal opinions about the [*Brown*] decision have no bearing on the matter of enforcement. . . . Mob rule cannot be allowed to override the decisions of our courts."[7]

The editors of the *New York Amsterdam News*, a newspaper geared toward the African American community, said of the President's decision:

> It is not too difficult for a man to stand up and fight for a cause with which he himself believes to be right. But it is quite another thing for a man to stand up and fight for a cause with which he himself does not agree but which he feels it is his duty to uphold.
>
> President Eisenhower is a battle-scarred veteran of many a campaign who has been hailed from one end of the world to the other. But we submit that his victory over himself at Little Rock was indeed his finest hour.[8]

In the weeks that followed, the 101st Airborne restored order in the streets. But neither the soldiers nor school officials had much effect on the small but determined group of white students who insulted, humiliated, and physically threatened the Little Rock Nine day after day. Still, all but one of the students made it through the year. And in May, Ernest Green became the first African American to graduate from Central High.

Singer Paul Robeson was one of many Americans who followed the crisis in Little Rock. In his autobiography, he says of Green and the other eight African American students:

> Dear children of Little Rock—you and your parents and the Negro people of your community have lifted our hearts and renewed our resolve that full freedom shall now be ours. . . . You are our children, but the peoples of the whole world rightly claim you, too. They have seen your faces, and the faces of those who hate you, and they are on your side. They see in you those qualities which parents everywhere want their children to have, and their best wishes. . . go out to you.

Yes, America—these are your children, too, you ought to be very proud of them. The American dream—the spirit of Jefferson and Lincoln, of Emerson and Twain—is given new life by the children of Little Rock. These children must ever be cherished, for they are not only the hope and the promise of my people: with them stands the destiny of democracy in America.[9]

Despite such praise at home and abroad, the crisis did not end with Green's graduation. Reporter Joan I. Duffy of the Memphis *Commercial Appeal*, explains:

That summer, Faubus and the segregationists had pushed through the legislature a new law allowing school districts to close schools rather than integrate.

The Little Rock School Board voted to close the city's four high schools for the 1958—1959 school year, sending thousands of families scrambling to find alternative education for their children. . . .

No one knows how many students, unable to find an alternative school after the closure, dropped out and never came back. Newspaper accounts at the time described a rash of moving vans taking families out of Little Rock in search of schools.

"Some 3,700 children of high school age have been affected by closings, 700 of them Negroes," a United Press International dispatch reported. . . .

Several churches cobbled together classes and a private, all-white school enrolled 917.

Closing the schools and the "purge" of 44 teachers by the school board for perceived support of integration ignited the outrage of Little Rock's moderates. They were led by 76-year-old Adolphine Fletcher Terry, a civically active society matron who had organized the city's public library system. She organized an army of 2,000 women—all of them white. By spring of 1959, a recall movement ousted three segregationists from the school board and replaced them with moderates. The schools re-opened in the fall of 1959.[10]

Rett Tucker, the president of the Chamber of Commerce, told Duffy, "Historians say that was the end of it, but you and I know we've been dealing with it ever since."[11]

CONNECTIONS

The nine African American students all lived in the Central High school district. As a result, they knew a number of white students in the school. Yet Elizabeth Eckford recalls, "Some of the students I'd known since I was 10 years old, who were white, were afraid to speak to me in school. It's true there were only about 50 students who were actively harassing us. But some of those other students, it was my feeling, were cooperating in that violence through their silence." How does one cooperate through silence? What is she suggesting about the role of the bystander?

What message were Hollingsworth's white neighbors sending when they closed their doors? To what extent were they cooperating in the violence?

There is an old saying that "Sticks and stones can break my bones but names can never hurt me." Is it true? What is the hurt that comes from words? from silence? from "just being ignored"? How might the situation at Central High School have been different if Webb and other white students had regarded black students as "kids" much like them?

As the mob harassed Elizabeth Eckford, Grace Lorch decided that she could not remain a bystander. She braved the crowd to help Eckford reach safety. The white ministers who accompanied the African American students to school that day also took a stand. How important were the choices they made to the black students? to the community as a whole? to themselves? What if others had supported the Little Rock Nine? For example, what if the principal or a group of teachers had opened the doors of the school and escorted the students into the building? How might that decision have altered the outcome of that day?

In 1957, Jesús Colón (Reading 3) wrote an article about the Little Rock Nine. In it, he describes what a friend did a few days after Faubus called out the National Guard.

Joe took a rough piece of paper from the factory and wrote a request to the President of the United States to use his federal and military powers to keep open the doors of the high school to the Negro children. Joe then asked the 60 workers in his shop to sign their names to the request. About 40 of them signed. Then Joe put the whole thing in an envelope and sent it to President Eisenhower. Joe is a white worker. Can you imagine the effect in the White House if other Joes in thousands of other factories and offices all over the nation would have done the same? Enough said.[12]

How would you answer Colón's question? How do you define the word *bystander*? Research suggests that the responses of bystanders give an event meaning. Television   dramatically increased the number of people who were bystanders to the riots in Little Rock. What is Colón suggesting about the ways they could give meaning to the event?

What do Doris Kearns Goodwin's remarks suggest about the way TV expanded her "universe of obligation"–the circle of individuals and groups "toward whom obligations are owed, to whom rules apply, and whose injuries call for [amends]"?[13] To what extent does TV expand your "universe of obligation"? The video *Eyes on the Prize*, available from the Facing History Resource Center, shows some of the images she saw on TV in 1957. How do those images help you understand why Goodwin views the crisis in Little Rock as a turning point in her political consciousness?

As governor of Arkansas, how did Orval Faubus define his "universe of obligation"? How did Eisenhower define his? Why did the editors of the *New York Amsterdam News* view Eisenhower's decision as "his finest hour"? What were they suggesting about the way a leader in a democracy defines his "universe of obligation"?

Harry Ashmore, the editor of the *Arkansas Gazette*, said of the crisis in Little Rock, "Orval Faubus was the hero to the mob; the nine courageous black children he failed to keep out of Central High were heroes to the world." To whom was Eisenhower a hero? How does Ashmore seem to define the word *hero*? How do you define it? Who do you think the heroes were in this story?

In 1955, Rosa Parks was arrested in Montgomery, Alabama, for refusing to move to the back of the bus as required by law. Her arrest prompted other African Americans to boycott the city buses. For twelve and a half months, under the leadership of Dr. Martin Luther King, Jr., they walked, carpooled, and rode in taxis rather than sit at the back of the bus. Their commitment inspired the Little Rock Nine. Melba Pattillo later wrote that she experienced a "surge of pride when I thought about how my people had banded together to force a change. It gave me hope that maybe things in Little Rock could change."[14] What connected African Americans in the two cities? How do you think the Little Rock Nine may be connected to students like Marian Wright Edelman, who registered black voters in the South or sat in at lunch counters in the 1960s? to those who took to the streets to demand laws that guaranteed equal rights for all Americans?

The Rev. Colbert Cartwright was one of the few white ministers to speak out against the mob. He and other religious leaders organized a day of prayer for peace in the city on October 12, 1957. Although more than 6,000 people participated, the next day the mob gathered once again outside Central High. And once again, other white citizens chose to look the other way. In reflecting on the crisis, Cartwright observed:

> In the end, the law could not [integrate the schools]. A group of very dedicated people, women. . . marshaled. . . grassroots support to take back the schools and work on the desegregation problem. The lesson is that people themselves had to take responsibility for what they wanted their community to be. . . . They had to rally the good forces in the community to take back the schools, do more than a lackluster desegregation effort by some edict. This was work that should have been done prior to desegregation.[15]

What is integration? What does he suggest is needed to integrate the schools?

 Listen to this audio:
ctp.facinghistory.org/stories/crisis_in_little_rock/in_her_own_words

[1] Marian Wright Edelman, *The Measure of Our Success: A Letter to My Children and Yours,* (Boston: Beacon Press, 1992), 5.

[2] David Halberstam, *The Fifties* (New York: Villard Books, 1993), 678.

[3] Doris Kearns Goodwin, *Wait Till Next Year* (New York: Simon and Schuster, 1997) 234.

[4] Ernest Green, *Voices of Freedom: An Oral History of the Civil Rights Movement from the 1950s through the 1980s,* edited by Henry Hampton and Steve Fayer (New York: Bantam Books, 1990) 39.

[5] Benjamin Fine, "Arkansas Troops Bar Negro Pupils; Governor Defiant" *New York Times,* September 5, 1957.

[6] Joan Duffy, "A Reunion with History: Central High will Observe 1957's Rite of Passage," *The Commercial Appeal,* September 21, 1997.

[7] President Dwight D. Eisenhower, "Mob Rule Cannot Be Allowed to Override the Decisions of Our Courts," September 24, 1957, *History Matters,* George Mason University website, http://historymatters.gmu.edu/d/6335/ (accessed on September 14, 2007).

[8] *New York Amsterdam News,* editorial, October 5, 1957.

[9] Paul Robeson, *Here I Stand* (Boston: Beacon Press, 1958), 109–10.

[10] Joan Duffy, "A Reunion with History: Central High will Observe 1957's Rite of Passage," *The Commercial Appeal,* September 21, 1997.

[11] Ibid.

[12] Jesús Colón, *The Way It Was and Other Writings* (Houston: Arte Público Press, 1993), 82.

[13] Helen Fein, *Accounting for Genocide* (London: The Free Press), 33.

[14] Melba Pattillo Beals, *Warriors Don't Cry: A Searing Memoir of the Battle to Integrate Little Rock's Central High* (New York: Pocket Books, 1994), 28.

[15] Sara Alderman Murphy, *Breaking the Silence* (Fayetteville: The University of Arkansas Press, 1997), 152.

In reflecting on what he learned from the crisis, the Rev. Colbert Cartwright observed, "The lesson is that people themselves had to take responsibility for what they wanted their community to be. To do so, they had to talk about the issues that divided them." Many Americans in the 1950s had never spoken at length to people from other ethnic and racial groups. Sociologist David Schoem has called that kind of isolation a "human and national tragedy"–one that encourages a "heavy reliance on stereotypes, gossip, rumor, and fear" to shape one's lack of knowledge.[1] How do people then or now break that isolation and learn to walk even briefly in someone else's shoes?

That was a question that few people in Little Rock or elsewhere asked in the 1950s. As a result, black and white students at Central High had few opportunities to express their fears, hopes, or concerns. They received dozens of memos from school officials urging them to be "good citizens." But their teachers avoided any discussion of what it meant to be a good citizen in Little Rock in 1957. In class, teachers followed the curriculum. They avoided talking about the mob outside the building or the harassment of the Little Rock Nine within.

The most famous photograph taken at Central High that year showed a white student screaming at Elizabeth Eckford on the day she confronted the mob. Elizabeth Huckaby, the vice-principal at Central High, said of the photo:

> No one seemed to be able to identify the girl–and small wonder. We were not used to seeing our students look like that. But by noon on Friday, I discovered she was someone I knew, and I sent for her in the afternoon. When she readily admitted she was the screaming girl, I told her how distressed I was to hear it since hatred destroys the people who hate. She shrugged. Well, that was the way she felt, she said. Undeterred by her shrug, I said that I hoped I'd never see her pretty face so distorted again, that I never would have recognized that ugly face in the picture as hers. Wasted breath.[2]

A few weeks later, NBC invited students at Central High to participate in a roundtable discussion moderated by Jorunn Ricketts. It was to be aired nationally. A close friend of the girl that Elizabeth Huckaby called into her office took part in that discussion. Her name was Sammy Dean Parker. The excerpt that follows focuses on Sammy's comments as well as those made by three other white students–Kay Bacon, Robin Woods, and Joe Fox–and two black students–Ernest Green and Minnijean Brown.

> MRS. RICKETTS: Do you think it is possible to start working this out on a more sensible basis than violent demonstration?
>
> SAMMY: No. I don't because the South has always been against racial mixing and I think they will fight this thing to the end. . . . We fight for our freedom–that's one thing. And we don't have any freedom anymore.
>
> ERNEST: Sammy, you say you don't have freedom. I wonder what you mean by it–that you don't have freedom? You are guaranteed your freedoms in the Bill of Rights and your Constitution. You have the freedom of speech–I noticed that has been exercised a whole lot in Little Rock. The freedom of petition, the freedom of religion, and the other freedoms are guaranteed to you. As far as freedom, I think that if anybody should kick about freedoms, it should be us. Because I think we have been given a pretty bad side on this thing as far as freedom.
>
> SAMMY: Do you call those troops freedom? I don't. And I also do not call it free when you are being escorted into the school every morning.

Hazel Bryan screams at Elizabeth Eckford, September 1957.

> ERNEST: You say, Why did the troops come here? It is because our government–our state government–went against the federal law. . . . Our country is set up so that we have 48 states and no one state has the ability to overrule our nation's government. I thought that was what our country was built around. I mean, that is why

we fight. We fought in World War II together–the fellows that I know died in World War II, they died in the Korean War. I mean, why should my friends go out there and die for a cause called "democracy" when I can't exercise my rights–tell me that. . . .

JOE: Well, Sammy, I don't know what freedom has been taken away from you because the truth is–I know as a senior myself–the troops haven't kept me from going to my classes or partici-pating in any school activity. I mean, they're there just to keep order in case–I might use the term "hotheads"–get riled up. But I think as long as–if parents would just stay out of it and let the children of the school at Central High figure it out for themselves, I think it would be a whole lot better. I think the students are mature enough to figure it out for themselves. . . . As far as I'm concerned, I'll lay the whole blame of this trouble in Governor Faubus's lap.

SAMMY: I think we knew before this ever started that someday we were going to have to integrate the schools. And I think our governor was trying to protect all of us when he called out the National Guard–and he was trying to prepare us, I think.

ERNEST: . . . Well, I have to disagree. . . . I know a student that's over there with us, Elizabeth [Eckford], and that young lady, she walked two blocks, I guess–as you all know–and the mob was behind her. Did the troops break up the mob?

ROBIN: . . . And when Elizabeth had to walk down in front of the school, I was there and I saw that. And may I say, I was very ashamed–I felt like crying–because she was so brave when she did that. And we just weren't behaving ourselves–just jeer-ing her. I think if we had had any sort of decency, we wouldn't have acted that way. But I think if everybody would just obey the Golden Rule–do unto others as you would have others do unto you–that might be the solution. How would you like to have to. . . walk down the street with everybody yelling behind you like they yelled behind Elizabeth?

MRS. RICKETTS: Sammy, why do these children not want to go to school with Negroes?

SAMMY: Well, I think it is mostly race mixing.

MRS. RICKETTS: Race mixing? What do you mean?

SAMMY: Well, marrying each other.

MINNIJEAN: Hold your hand up. I'm brown, you are white. What's the difference? We are all of the same thoughts. You're thinking about your boy–he's going to the Navy. I'm thinking about mine–he's in the Air Force. We think about the same thing.

SAMMY: I'll have to agree with you. . . .

MINNIJEAN: Kay, Joe, and Robin–do you know anything about me, or is it just that your mother has told you about Negroes?

MRS. RICKETTS: . . . Have you ever really made an effort to find out what they're like?

KAY: Not until today.

SAMMY: Not until today.

MRS. RICKETTS: And what do you think about it after today?

KAY: Well, you know that my parents and a lot of the other students and their parents think the Negroes aren't equal to us. But–I don't know. It seems like they are, to me.

SAMMY: These people are–we'll have to admit that.

ERNEST: I think, like we're doing today, discussing our different views. . . . If the people of Little Rock. . .would get together, I believe they would find out a different story–and try to discuss the thing instead of getting out in the street and kicking people around and calling names–and that sort of thing.   If. . .people got together it would be smoothed over.

KAY: I think that if. . . our friends had been getting in this discussion today, I think that maybe some of them–not all of them–in time, they would change their mind. But probably some of them would change their mind today.[3]

After the roundtable discussion, life at Central High went on much as it had before. A small group of white students continued to harass the Little Rock Nine, while the majority looked the other way. Still there were a few signs of change. Terrence Roberts, one of the Little Rock Nine, was assigned to Robin Woods's algebra class. Realizing he didn't have a math book, she made "a gut-level decision" and pulled her desk over to his so they could share her book. There was "a gasp of disbelief." For the rest of the year, segregationists harassed Woods and her family.

Teachers and other school officials never found a way to stop the torment of the African American students or the few white students brave enough to befriend them. By November, Minnijean Brown had had enough. She retaliated while standing in the lunch line one day. Ernest Green recalls:

> Minnie was about five foot ten and this fellow couldn't have been more than five-five, five-four. He reminded me of a small dog, yelping at somebody's leg. Minnie had just picked up her chili, and before I could even say, "Minnie, why don't you tell him to shut up?" Minnie had taken this chili and dumped it on this dude's head. There was absolute silence in the place, and then the help, all black, broke into applause. And the other white kids there didn't know what to do. It was the first time that anybody, I'm sure, had seen somebody black retaliate in that sense.[4]

Minnijean Brown was suspended for six days. Soon after the incident, a white student dumped a bowl of hot soup on her. He was suspended for two days. Then in February, Brown once again responded–this time verbally–to harassment by a white student. She was expelled for the rest of the year. She said of the incident:

> I just can't take everything they throw at me without fighting back.

> I don't think people realize what goes on at Central. You just wouldn't believe it. They throw rocks, they spill ink on your clothes, they call you "nigger," they just keep bothering you every five minutes.

> The white students hate me. Why do they hate me so much?

Northern civil rights activists arranged for Brown to attend Lincoln High School in New York City. `Even though white students openly distributed cards that read "One down, eight to go," the other eight African American students finished out the school year.

That summer, with the support of Governor Faubus and the state legislature, the Little Rock School Board closed all of the city's high schools–the three "white high schools" and the one "black school." Earlier that year, most white students and their parents saw themselves as bystanders. Now they discovered that they were deeply involved in the crisis. A number of parents began to speak out. A few organized to reopen the city's high schools to both black and white students. Among them was Sara Alderman Murphy. Her experience convinced her that "Little Rock was split into two communities that did not communicate or know enough about each other to solve problems together."[5] She decided that "work needed to be done in changing attitudes–my own as well as others'."[6]

In 1963, she organized an interfaith, interracial group of women willing to speak about "race" to civic clubs, religious groups, and women's organizations in Little Rock and beyond. One evening, Mildred Terry, an elementary school teacher and a member of Murphy's group, told a white audience about her son Alvin. He was one of the first black students at a local junior high school. She described how he was punched in the back, knocked down stairs, and repeatedly called names by white students at the school. After the program, a white boy asked to speak with her. She later shared that conversation with Murphy:

> When he and Terry were alone, he said: "You don't know me but you would if I told you my name. I was one of those boys who harassed Alvin. I hadn't thought about how it made him feel until I heard you talking today. Please tell him I'm sorry I did it."
>
> "I certainly did remember his name when he gave it," Terry said later, laughing. "He made Alvin's life miserable but I can't get over what he said today. I was really moved to know he finally understood what he had done."[7]

CONNECTIONS

The roundtable discussion organized by NBC was one of the few opportunities Central High students had to talk about their concerns. In that conversation, students raised all of the issues that were part of the debate on integration–questions of equality vs. states' rights, fear of "race mixing," and the conflict between free speech and free association and individual rights. None of these issues were discussed at school. How do you think the students learned about them? What did the roundtable discussion add to their understanding of these issues? To the understanding of those who heard their discussion?

Suppose a community group, the school, or the students themselves had organized informal conversations like NBC's roundtable discussion. Who might have benefited? What might the students have learned from one another? How important is that learning? How else can individuals and groups bridge the differences that separate them?

Hazel Bryan was the student who screamed at Elizabeth Eckford the day she confronted the mob. In 1962, five years later, Bryan apologized to Eckford. Bryan later said:

> I don't know what triggered it, but one day I just started squall-ing about how she must have felt. I felt so bad that I had done this that I called her. . . and apologized to her. I told her I was sorry that I had done that, that I was not thinking for myself. . . . I think both of us were crying.[8]

What do you think may have prompted Bryan's apology? How important was the apology to Eckford? to Bryan?

Robin Woods says she made a "gut-level" decision to help Terrence Roberts. What is a "gut-level" decision? What risks did Woods take? Would her decision have been different if the newcomer had been a white student? How do you think she feels today about the choice she made then? How did she learn empathy? How have you learned to see others as sufficiently like yourself that you regard them as worthy of tolerance and respect? What experiences have helped you to understand other points of view? What experiences have had the opposite effect?

Daisy Bates, president of the Arkansas NAACP, said of the teachers in the school:

> Many of the teachers—particularly the younger ones—did everything within their power to protect the nine students. Some went out of their way to help the students catch up with work they had missed when they were barred from entering the school in the first weeks of the term. Concerned over the lack of protection given the Negro students within the school, the teachers took it upon themselves to oversee the hallways in between the class breaks.[9]

At the end of the school year, the Little Rock School Board fired 44 teachers for perceived support of integration. How does the board's action complicate your understanding of the silence within Central High?

The editors of the *New York Post* said of the punishment school officials gave Minnijean Brown, "When a Negro girl is so drastically penalized for reacting as a human being under fire, it is no wonder that white youngsters in the school feel safe to resume the business of bullying."[10] What part did white parents and other adults play in the crisis in Little Rock? To what extent did their choices encourage harassment of the Little Rock Nine? To what extent did their choices encourage other white students to remain bystanders? What does it take to stand up to a bully? Is standing up to a bully a heroic act?

In an editorial, the *New York Post* compared and contrasted New York City and Little Rock by focusing on what Minnijean Brown would discover when she came North:

> Minnijean will find the [racial] demarcation line here less obvious. But part of the education she gets in Our Town will be the knowledge that we too practice racial discrimination, though more subtly than the folks back home. We hope it doesn't come as too much of a shock to her to discover the difference between New York and Little Rock is not as great as it should be. Possibly her arrival will inspire us to be worthy of her and the cause for which she and other Southern Negro children have stood so stoically and so valiantly. Little Rock's loss is our proud acquisition.[11]

What are the editors suggesting about the similarities between New York and Little Rock? about the differences between the two cities? about the differences between the North and South? Find out about the way schools in your community handled racial differences. What does your research suggest about the similarities and differences between your community and Little Rock?

In 1957, Doris Kearns Goodwin attended high school in Rockville Centre, New York. She had two teachers who "thought much more could be learned from the drama in Arkansas than from the prescribed textbooks."[12] In both her social studies and English classes, those teachers challenged her biases and encouraged her to think independently. They were teaching her how to be a citizen in a democracy. How is democracy taught in your school today? How are you learning to be a citizen in a democracy?

Doris Kearns Goodwin's high school in Rockville Centre was more than a thousand miles from the mob that gathered outside Central High. How do you think distance affected the choices teachers made during the crisis? What other factors may have encouraged silence in Little Rock and discussion in Rockville Centre?

In 1997, when Elizabeth Eckford was asked why she returned to Central High after her experience with the mob, she replied, "Somewhere along the line, very soon [staying at Central] became an obligation. I realized that what we were doing was not for ourselves." What was that obligation? For whom do you think she and the others were enduring the harassment, if not for themselves? What does Sara Murphy's story suggest about the way communities can break isolation? About the way we as individuals expand our "universe of obligation"?

In September of 1997, U.S. News & World Report described Central High School today.

> In some ways, Central High stands as a model of desegrega-
> tion's success. The once all-white student body is now 58 per-
> cent black and 39 percent white. The school produces many of
> the state's brightest students, black and white, and sends them
> on to the nation's best universities. Over the past decade, of
> Arkansas's 32 black National Merit semifinalists, 15 have come
> from Central High. . . .[13]

The article notes that the honors classes at the school are mainly white, and the regular classes are primarily black. The reporters found that no one knew why this was so. Some thought it was due to racism. Others attributed it to the poor academic preparation of incoming black students or to socioeconomic conditions. The article went on to say:

> The racial makeup of classrooms reinforces self-segregation in other parts of school life. Most black students walk or take the bus to school and enter through the school's front doors. Most white students drive cars and come in a side door near the parking lot. Most black students eat lunch inside, near the hot lunch line, while white students eat outside, near the concession stand.
>
> And even though most Central High students generally say they have friends of different races, they acknowledge that for the most part they hang out with friends from their neighborhood, their junior high, or their classes.[14]

What does the article suggest about the progress Central High has made since 1957? the progress Little Rock and the nation have made? What does it suggest about the work that remains to be done? Who is responsible for making those changes?

In 1997, at the 40th anniversary of the integration of Central High, Mike Huckabee, the Republican governor of Arkansas, told the Little Rock Nine and the world:

> Today we come to say once and for all that what happened here 40 years ago was simply wrong. It was evil, and we renounce it. What the people did who tried to hold those nine from entering the doors of this high school is forgivable, but it is not excusable.[15]

How important was it that the governor acknowledge that a wrong had been done to the Little Rock Nine? How important was it that he renounce those wrongs even though they took place when someone else was governor? To what extent do such actions affect healing? reconciliation? education?

Watch this video:
www.facinghistory.org/video/terrence-roberts-la

[1] *Inside Separate Worlds: Life Stories of Young Blacks, Jews, and Latinos*, edited by David Schoem (Ann Arbor: University of Michigan Press, 1991), 3.

[2] Elizabeth Huckaby, *Crisis at Central High: Little Rock 1957–58* (Baton Rouge: Louisiana State University Press, 1980), 24.

[3] "Integration: Central Students Talk it Out," *New York Times*, October 20, 1957.

[4] Ernest Green, *Voices of Freedom: An Oral History of the Civil Rights Movement from the 1950s through the 1980s*, edited by Henry Hampton and Steve Fayer (New York: Bantam Books, 1990) 49–50.

[5] Sara Alderman Murphy, *Breaking the Silence* (Fayetteville: The University of Arkansas Press, 1997), 244.

[6] Ibid., 237.

[7] Ibid., 246–7.

[8] Ibid., 58.

[9] Daisy Bates, *The Long Shadow of Little Rock* (Fayetteville: The University of Arkansas Press, 1997), 144–45.

[10] *The New York Post*, February 19, 1958.

[11] Ibid.

[12] Doris Kearns Goodwin, *Wait Till Next Year* (New York: Simon & Schuster, 1997), 233.

[13] Julian E. Barnes, "Segregation, Now," *U.S. News & World Report*, September 22, 1997.

[14] Ibid.

[15] Governor Mike Huckabee, "Never again be silent when people's rights are at stake," September 26, 1997, *Arkansas Online*, http://www.ardemgaz.com/prev/central/govtext26.html (accessed on August 7, 2007).

Sargent Shriver dreamed big. Even before Little Rock, he believed in the power of government to improve the lives of ordinary citizens. As a member of the Kennedy family, one of the most powerful political families in the United States, Shriver both challenged and inspired ordinary Americans and their elected officials to think about the role of the government as a force for democratic change.

Shriver's parents founded the influential Catholic magazine *Commonweal.* Shriver took up journalism as well. He was already a successful magazine editor by the time he married Eunice Kennedy, the sister of the future president. The narrator of the documentary *The American Idealist* explains that Shriver "knew he was entering a powerful

Shriver strongly believed in the potential of people otherwise viewed as invisible members of society—foreigners, the uneducated, the poor.

family, but in the early 1950s, few would have predicted how powerful it would become. Each son to be a senator, each, to run for president."[1]

As a young man, Shriver became president of the Board of Education in Chicago. He also led a Catholic civil rights organization that pressured Catholic hospitals and schools to desegregate. Shriver's successes made him a rising star in Illinois and people began to discuss a possible run for governor. Shriver put his own ambition on hold when Eunice's brother, New York Senator John Fitzgerald Kennedy, decided to seek the Democratic nomination for president. Shriver agreed to join the campaign.

In his role as an adviser, Shriver pressed John Kennedy to speak out on civil rights and to support civil rights leader Rev. Martin Luther King, Jr. For him, these were not simply political issues, they were moral issues as well. Shriver's biographer Scott Stossel explains, "What drove him was this underlying concern with achieving racial and social justice and eradicating what he felt was the sin of racism."[2]

At a campaign stop at the University of Michigan, John Kennedy issued a challenge to the 10,000 students who had gathered to hear him speak. He asked: "How many of you who are going to be doctors are willing to spend your days in Ghana? Technicians or engineers, how many of you are willing to work in the Foreign Service and spend your lives traveling around the world? On your willingness... to contribute part of your life to this country, I think will depend the answer whether a free society can compete."[3]

In response, 800 students at the University of Michigan signed a petition pledging to volunteer. In return, Kennedy announced that if elected, he would create a Peace Corps. After Kennedy's narrow victory, he assigned Shriver to make what had started as campaign rhetoric a reality. Kennedy envisioned a small program, but Shriver had bigger plans. For him, the Peace Corps would provide an outlet for the goodwill of young citizens hoping to make a difference around the world. In the middle of the Cold War, Shriver believed the Peace Corps could offer a democratic answer to the appeal of communism. Despite Kennedy's reservations about Shriver's ambitious plans, Shriver was able to convince Congress to support his program. Within two years, the Peace Corps signed up more than 10,000 volunteers who worked in 43 different countries, teaching, building schools, and staffing hospitals.

After John Kennedy's assassination in 1963, Lyndon Johnson became president. Johnson turned to Shriver to run another program, the War on Poverty. While the battles over civil rights were being fought, the president felt that there was a need to focus on the economic conditions that he believed stood in the way of citizens' ability to enjoy their newly protected civil rights. The War on Poverty would become a centerpiece of Johnson's legislative agenda to fulfill his vision of "the Great Society."

Stossel describes the enormous challenge that Shriver was asked to take on:

> If a general was asked, you know, I want you to launch a war on Grenada, could you invade it and take it over, well you know that's something you can get your mind around. But, a war on poverty? That's like saying could you. . . wage war on gravity?[4]

Shriver began by learning what he could. He traveled the country–from Appalachia, to the Deep South, to ghettos in the North–to learn about what author Michael Harrington called "the Other America," or the invisible poor. The War on Poverty would be coordinated through the Office of Economic Opportunity (OEO). The narrator of *The American Idealist* explains, "As in the Peace Corps, he wanted the poor to lift themselves out of poverty and he wanted privileged Americans to work among them."[5] Among the many different initiatives, OEO created Volunteers in Service To America (VISTA), Head Start, the Youth Corps, the Job Corps, and a program called Community Action designed to help develop and sustain programs designed by poor people to meet their own needs. For Shriver, creating opportunities for citizens was the purpose of government. When asked by a cynical reporter, "Mr. Shriver, do you really believe that poverty can be wiped out?" Shriver answered without a moment's hesitation, "Yes, I do."[6]

At a commencement speech for the students of St. John's University in the spring of 1965, Shriver urged young people to get involved in what he called "the politics of service"[7]:

> Symbolically, the rest of your lives will be spent. . . in trying to establish a relationship between that name on your diploma and the world about you–step-by-step–in an ever-widening geographical and spiritual orbit.
>
> Names, words, terms, jargons–the things you hate learned by rote–that you have been schooled to spew back at just the right moment in just the right way–they must become real. . . . And in becoming real, they will change both you–and the world around you.
>
> We have a saying. . . in the Peace Corps. . . . "If you want to change the world, start small."
>
> For it is only in the context of the concrete, the immediate, even the trivial that the big words–words like justice and opportunity and humanity–will take on meaning. . . .
>
> Step by step, proceeding from the tangible, the small, and the immediate–we will learn at once the oldest and newest of

meanings for words that have lost all meaning.

Take words like civil rights, or equal or racial discrimination. Did we, as a nation, really understand what those words meant until demonstrations brought us into contact with concrete instances where Negro patrons were allowed to purchase food, but not to eat it on the premises or where they were allowed to eat it standing up, but not sitting down or to eat it at the stool counter, but not in booths? Or another instance. . . where a drugstore would not serve Negroes Coca-Cola, even though it would serve them Pepsi-Cola?

It is when we begin with the trivial—the small, when our sense of injustice is engaged and aroused—that equality takes on meaning and we seize what President Johnson has called: "the glorious opportunity of this generation. . . to find America for ourselves with the same immense thrill of discovery which gripped those who first began to realize that there, at last, was a home for freedom."

The same sense of discovery, of renewal is there—waiting—in the War Against Poverty.

. . . The reality of terms, words, names, comes out of particulars, directly experienced—irrevocably experienced.

. . . The geography lesson does not stop at the U.S. border.[8]

Shriver describes how the experiences of young people in the Peace Corps, working outside the United States, challenges them to rethink what it means to be an American. That question, Shriver suggests, is tied to another question. He asks, What does it mean to be a citizen of the world? For Shriver, the answers will come from working with the other. He explains:

. . .You must learn to see teachers, new teachers where others have seen only foreigners, peasants, backward natives, hillbillies, Negroes, Indians, poor white trash and even the so-called culturally deprived.[9]

Shriver strongly believed that "Built into each individual's experience must be an occasion for giving, a task of humanity, an act of sharing and sacrifice."[10]

It was that fundamental principle that connected the Peace Corps with the War on Poverty. Both programs gave ordinary people a chance to express their own idealism while learning through firsthand experience. Government programs for Shriver were about building sustainable democracy, either through offering people a chance to learn new skills or by providing the key services that would enable people to stand up for themselves. During the first year of the War on Poverty, the program reached three million people. *Newsweek* proclaimed, "The poor were no longer invisible."[11]

The most controversial aspects of Shriver's War on Poverty were programs that directly empowered community groups independently of local government intervention. For Shriver, it was essential to find ways to help poor people use their power to challenge "hostile or uncaring institutions. . .especially government."[12] Key to that struggle was creating a program of legal services for poor people. With the help of legal services, poor people were able to hold both the government and employers accountable to the law. On the defensive, many state and local officials objected to the plan, arguing that Shriver was giving money to people who in turn took the government to court. Shriver remained defiant. He explained:

> We expect action at the community level. And when you've got action, you've got dissent [and] you've got differences of opinion. . . . For the first time in the history of this country, poor people actually have a place and a way to express themselves. . . . We're creating life at the community level, and when you've got life you've got movement, you've got dissension, you've got action, that's what we want.[13]

Organizer and activist Marian Wright Edelman describes the impact of one of the local initiatives, the Child Development Group of Mississippi: "Mississippi in the mid 1960s when the poverty program began was virtually a slavery system where people worked all year and lived and bought their food from the plantation owner and at the end of the year they found they owed him money. . . . Black children had no fair opportunity."

Edelman testifies that the program began to make an impact. She explains, "It was a revolution in many ways both economically and for the parents'. . . vision of themselves and hopes that their children can be different than they."[14]

The program faced a strong backlash from people who wished to maintain the status quo. Working inside the Johnson administration, Shriver had to be careful to maintain the support of Congress and of the president. Sometimes Shriver found himself caught between the politicians in Washington who feared that his programs were causing trouble and the poor people he hoped to serve, who felt that he compromised too much.

During the late 1960s, the War on Poverty found itself competing with the war in Vietnam for funding. As the Vietnam War continued, President Johnson's popularity waned. Riots after the assassination of Martin Luther King, Jr. in April 1968 further polarized the nation. Just two months later, Democratic presidential candidate Robert F. Kennedy, Shriver's brother-in-law and a vocal advocate for the poor, was killed shortly after winning the California primary.

After Richard M. Nixon's victory in the 1968 elections, Shriver left public office but he continued to be a force in politics, running for vice president in 1972 and for president in 1976. He found other ways to participate as well. A devout Catholic, Shriver worked with the leaders of the U.S. Catholic Church to create a pastoral letter warning against the dangers of nuclear weapons. In 1986, he became president of the Special Olympics–an idea that originated with his wife Eunice's day camp for children with intellectual disabilities held at their family home.

Looking back on Shriver's record, many historians note, "From 1964 to 1968, nearly one out of every three poor Americans left the poverty rolls. It was the largest four-year drop ever recorded."[15] Historians agree that the War on Poverty was one of several factors that contributed to the dramatic drop.

Today, many programs Shriver initiated continue to serve the community, including the Head Start early education programs. Since its inception, Head Start has educated more than 23 million children. At the same time, the Peace Corps continues to attract people from all over the United States looking to make a difference. Since 1961, 200,000 Peace Corps volunteers have served abroad. Many people understand that Shriver's legacy is bigger than the numbers. For many, Shriver represents a spirit of idealism and hope in the power of the government to improve people's lives. Longtime Shriver friend and adviser Edgar May declares, "You can denigrate that. . . .

You can be cynical. But look around. We're still a country of optimists–we're still a country of young people who want to make a contribution . . . and that same spirit, that same need for the human being to do something larger for herself, for himself–to prove their humanity–that same need exists today."[16]

CONNECTIONS

This reading is based on the documentary film *American Idealist,* which tells the story of Shriver's life and offers details about his work, including sections on civil rights, the Peace Corps, and the War on Poverty. The film, which can be used to complement this reading, includes compelling footage and engaging interviews. Copies of the film are available from the Facing History and Ourselves resource library.

What is an idealist? How does idealism shape the way people think about the world around them? The opposite of an idealist is a cynic. What is a cynic? How does cynicism shape the way people think about possibilities for change?

Journalist Bill Moyers remembers how Shriver worked to build support for the Peace Corps in Congress. Shriver would ask Congress members, "Don't you believe in young people? Don't you believe in American idealism? Don't you believe we've got a new mission in the world?"[17] How do you imagine Congress members responded to his questions? how would you respond? What do you think Shriver felt was the mission of the United States in the world? do you share that same vision? Explain.

Shriver recounts a saying in the Peace Corps: "If you want to change the world, start small." What does that mean in practice? Think of a problem that you would like to change and break it down into small steps. How would you begin? Which approach is most likely to lead to success? If you start small, how can you ensure that you are able to address the roots of the problem?

Shriver talked about the "politics of service." What did he mean? What opportunities have you had to participate in creating positive change?

Shriver believed that to help make a difference in people's lives you had to walk in somebody else's shoes. He explained that that part of learning comes from the ability to "see teachers. . .where others have seen only foreigners, peasants, backward natives, hillbillies, Negroes, Indians, poor white trash, and even the so-called culturally deprived." Have you ever tried to walk in somebody else's shoes? What did you learn from the experience? What allows people to "see teachers" where others have seen only the "culturally deprived"? Who are the people who have taught you lessons about life?

One goal of the War on Poverty was community action. In fact, many scholars believe that a good way to measure the strength of a democracy is to examine the level of participation by ordinary citizens in their community and the world. What opportunities are there for civic participation in your community?

Critics charged some of Shriver's programs with stirring up trouble by empowering people to stand up for their rights and demand political change. To what extent should a democracy protect the right to dissent? To what extent should it encourage it?

Shriver said, "For it is only in the context of the concrete, the immediate, even the trivial, that the big words–words like *justice* and *opportunity* and *humanity*–will take on meaning." What does he mean? Can you give an example?

Shriver thinks that certain words like "civil rights" and "racial discrimination" have lost their meaning. Why do words lose their meaning? What is lost when words become meaningless? How does he think they will regain their meaning?

 Watch this video:
www.americanidealistmovie.com/videoClip5.htm

---

[1] *American Idealist: The Story of Sargent Shriver*, DVD (Chicago: Chicago Video Project, 2006).

[2] Ibid.

[3] Remarks of Senator John F. Kennedy, University of Michigan, October 14, 1960, http://www.jfklibrary.org/Historical+Resources/JFK+in+History/Peace+Corps.htm (accessed on August 21, 2007).

[4] *American Idealist*, DVD.

[5] Ibid.

[6] Ibid.

[7] Ibid.

[8] "Address by Sargent Shriver," St. John's University, Jamaica, NY, June 13, 1965, http://www.sargentshriver.com/medium_file/file/2206/1965_-_ST_JOHN_S_UNIVERSITY.pdf (accessed on July 16, 2007).

[9] Ibid.

[10] Ibid.

[11] *American Idealist*, DVD.

[12] Ibid.

[13] Ibid.

[14] Ibid.

[15] Ibid.

[16] Ibid.

[17] Ibid.

The decade of the 1960s was marked by turmoil in the United States–much of it racially motivated. Although many groups and individuals still struggle for dignity, respect, and rights today, a great deal has changed since the 1960s, as demonstrated by the election of the first African American US president in 2008. Resistance to social change is often expressed through hatred and violence. How a community responds to intolerance is one measure of its citizens' commitment to democracy.

During the early 1990s, hate groups in Billings, Montana organized a wave of racist and antisemitic violence. In 1994 journalist Claire Safran reported on the community's response.

On a quiet evening in Billings, Montana, early [in December 1993], a stranger arrived at the home of Tammie and Brian Schnitzer. He stole across the lawn, a cinder block in hand. He stopped at a window decorated with Star of David decals and a menorah, the nine-branched candelabra that is the symbol of the Jewish festival of Chanukah. Then he hurled the stone, sending jagged shards of glass into the bedroom of Isaac, 5.

Members of the Billings Painters Union volunteer to repaint a neighbor's home defaced by racist graffitti.

By chance, the little boy wasn't there. He'd been in the family room watching TV with his 2-year-old sister, Rachel, and a babysitter. They heard the crash, but when the sitter searched for a cause, she missed the broken window. That remained for Brian to find when he came home. Shaken, he phoned the police and put the children to bed in the safest spot he could think of–bundled in sleeping bags under the four-poster bed in his bedroom. "We're playing campout," he told Isaac.

Not long after, Tammie returned from a meeting of the human rights coalition she co-chaired. Seeing the look on her husband's face, she asked, "What's wrong?" He led her to Isaac's room. Shocked, she stared at the broken window. Tammie had felt a little nervous putting up the Chanukah decorations; in recent months, a string of hate crimes had occurred around town. Now her worst fears had come home.

Waiting for the police to arrive, Tammie huddled in a rocking chair in her son's room. "I felt so cold," she recalls. "But it wasn't the winter air coming through the broken window. It was my sense of being so helpless. It was my fear of what would come next."

Some 80,000 people live under the big sky of this valley town sheltered by rocky hills. They drive pickups and family sedans, dress in jeans and business suits, and mingle in an easy, relaxed way. They are overwhelmingly Christian and white; about 50 Jewish families live here, and fewer than 500 blacks. Add Hispanics and Native Americans, [and] all told, minorities in Billings make up a meager 7 percent or so of the population.

For some that's still too many. In 1986 white supremacists declared Montana to be one of five states comprising their "Aryan homeland." In the years that followed, racist incidents around the state became increasingly frequent; eventually they cropped up in Billings. . . .

By the end of 1992, the Knights of the Ku Klux Klan and a band of skinheads had become visible presences in Billings. Klan newspapers were tossed onto driveways, and flyers surfaced attacking mainly Jews and homosexuals. One day a bumper sticker that read "Nuke Israel" was placed on a stop sign near the temple. Not long after, Tammie saw a flyer that named Brian, who'd recently become president of the Montana association of Jewish Communities. "I felt sick," she recalls. "It really hit home."

At a meeting, temple officers chose not to speak out. Says Tammie, "They seemed to feel that to acknowledge a problem or identify ourselves as being different would make us stand apart." Tammie refused to stay silent. . . .

At the same time, Margaret MacDonald . . . a mother of two and the part-time director of the Montana Association of Churches, was encountering resistance to another effort to draw attention to the problem: a petition that opposed hatred and bigotry. "There'd been an emphatic hard-line stance in the town, like a brick wall, that the less said about the skinheads and other racists, the better," she says. She persisted, however, and over the following months, more than 100 organizations and 3,500 people signed the resolution.

In the spring of 1993, after a conversation at a town meeting, Tammie, Margaret, and several others formed the Billings Coalition for Human Rights. "This wasn't a Jewish issue, it was a human rights issue," says Tammie. "We wanted to make the community aware of what was going on."

The hate activity escalated. In September, four days before the start of the Jewish New Year, vandals overturned headstones in the Jewish cemetery. And on the holiday itself, a bomb threat was made to the temple before the start of the children's service.

Tammie urged synagogue members to speak out. "I wanted to let people know what was happening. But some members felt that we would put ourselves in more danger. We didn't know what to do."

In the weeks that followed, several Billings residents–inspired by the Coalition for Human Rights–took action against racism. When skinheads showed up at services of the African Methodist Episcopal Wayman Chapel, small groups of white Christians appeared in response. They sat with the congregation until the skinheads stopped coming. In October an interracial couple awoke one morning to find crude words and a swastika spray-painted on their house. Three days later, volunteers from the local painters union repaired the damage.

But with the arrival of the holiday season, the hate incidents turned violent. In late November a beer bottle was thrown through the window of a Jewish home. And then, on the night of December 2, the Schnitzer home was attacked.

As Tammie spoke with the police officer who'd arrived at her home, she swung between fear and outrage. "This isn't just mischief," she said. He agreed and advised her to take down the Chanukah decorations and avoid leaving the children with a babysitter.

Lying in bed that night, sleepless, Tammie thought how ironic it was that the attack on her home had occurred because of Chanukah—a holiday commemorating the Jews' fight thousands of years ago to worship God in their own way. "I wondered what kind of struggle we were going to be in for, and how we could stop it before it became worse," she says.

The next day, Friday, Tammie spoke with a reporter from the Billings Gazette. She told him how troubled she was by the officer's advice. "Maybe it's not wise to keep these symbols up," she said. "But how do you explain that to a child?"

On Saturday morning Margaret [MacDonald] read Tammie's quote in the paper. She tried to imagine telling her daughter, Siri, then 6, that they could not have a Christmas tree, or explaining to Charlie, then 3, that they had to take a wreath off the door because it wasn't safe.

Margaret phoned her pastor, Keith Torney. "What would you think if we had the children draw menorahs in Sunday school?" she asked. "If we mimeographed as many pictures of the menorah as we could? If we told people to put them up in their windows?"

Reverend Torney had read the paper that morning too. "Yes," he said. "And yes again." He spent the rest of the day on the phone, enlisting other churches. That week hundreds of menorahs appeared in the windows of Christian homes in Billings. "It wasn't an easy decision," says Margaret. "With two young children, I had to think hard about it myself. We put our menorah in a living room window, and made sure nobody sat in front of it."

One of the first to put up a menorah was Becky Thomas, . . . a Catholic mother of two who lives near the Schnitzers. "It's easy to go around saying you support some good cause, but this was different. It was putting ourselves in danger," she says. "I told my husband, 'Now we know how the Schnitzers feel.'"

Some, nervous about jeopardizing their families, checked first with Wayne Inman, the chief of police at the time. "Yes, there's a risk," he told callers. "But there's a greater risk in not doing it."

On December 7, the Billings Gazette published a full-page picture of a menorah to cut out and tape up. Local businesses also distributed photocopies of menorahs, and one put a message on a billboard, proclaiming: "Not in Our Town! No Hate, No Violence. Peace on Earth."

As the Jewish symbol sprouted in Christian windows, the haters lashed out. Glass panes on the doors of the Evangelical United Methodist Church, graced with two menorahs, were smashed. Someone fired shots into a Catholic school that had joined the crusade. Six cars parked in front of homes that displayed menorahs had their windows kicked out; the homeowners received phone calls that told them to "Go look at your car, Jew-lover."

Yet suddenly, for every menorah that was there before, ten new ones appeared. Hundreds of menorahs grew to be thousands. It's estimated that as many as 6,000 homes in Billings had menorahs on display. "All along, our coalition had been saying an attack on one of us is an attack on all of us," says Margaret MacDonald. "And God bless them, the people of this town understood." . . .

The people of Billings kept their menorahs up until the New Year. As Inman says, "The haters could attack a couple of Jewish homes. They could make a second wave of attacks on Christian homes and churches. But they could not target thousands of menorahs."

Confronted by a united town, the Ku Klux Klan and skinheads backed off. The acts of vandalism stopped, the hate literature disappeared, and the anonymous calls ended. But with no witnesses and no strong leads, the police were never able to make any arrests, a fact that leaves the community extremely uneasy. . . .

The town continues to stand together. In April [of 1994] more than 250 Christians joined the Jewish community for a seder, the traditional Passover meal. Not long after, hundreds attended a concert of Jewish music that the Schnitzers helped coordinate to show their appreciation to Billings.

Tammie Schnitzer and Margaret MacDonald are busy organizing meetings and speaking at schools about racial sensitivity. With Chanukah just a few weeks away, they're stepping up their activities and are working on combined holiday events for the temple and local churches.

Soon Tammie's going to be putting up her Chanukah decorations. "I have to make sure my kids are proud of themselves and never have to hide who they are," she says. "Yes, I'm afraid. But I know if something happened again, the community would respond."

Becky Thomas, for one, is prepared. "We saved our menorah, and it's going in our window again," she says. "We need to show commitment for a lifetime."[1]

Roger Rosenblatt of *The New York Times* interviewed Billings residents in 1994 and found that many of them were reassessing their attitudes and beliefs as a result of the menorah campaign. Wayne Inman, former Billings chief of police, told Rosenblatt that although there were no African Americans or Jews in his hometown, he grew up hearing racial slurs.

It was as common as the sun coming up in the morning. Nobody ever confronted the issue. It was "normal." But when I got out into the larger world, I found that it wasn't normal, or if it was normal, it should be opposed. When you have a person present, not just a word, you see that you're talking about a human being whose skin is black. I saw that for myself. I saw the hurt and pain in his eyes. It became a very personal issue for me.[2]

Some in the community wondered whether a black or Hispanic family would have received similar community support. (The Schnitzers are Jewish, but they are also white, middle-class citizens.) Others felt that putting up a menorah was "relatively painless for the community." Rosenblatt goes on to note:

> There is discussion, as well, about the difference between encouraging diversity in the community and opposing bigotry. Several evangelical churches did not participate in the menorah movement because it was led by the Human Rights Coalition, whose support of homosexual rights they do not endorse. . . . "Once there was a visual act of bigotry, it was easy to get people involved," [Kurt] Nelson says. "Personal tolerance is harder to achieve. . . ."[3]

Sarah Anthony, a member of the Human Rights Coalition, reflected on the struggle and why it matters to her. She told Rosenblatt:

> I mean, what have we done so far? Come up with a plan. Make a few phone calls. Put up menorahs. That's all we did. Pretty simple stuff, actually. But you have to build the sentiment, to forge the real feeling that goes deep. We did something right here, and we will do it again if we have to. If we don't, there are people who would break every window in Billings, and we would look out those windows and see ourselves.[4]

Documentary filmmaker Patrice O'Neill captured the story of Billings in "Not In Our Town." By showing how a community can respond to hate, the half-hour documentary sparked a national and international movement of individuals, schools, and communities organizing grassroots events, educational outreach, and public dialogue. The film's title has become a motto for those seeking to stand up to racism, bigotry, and intimidation. O'Neill says that she has been taken aback by the response to the film:

> The Not In Our Town Project and the Billings story has been one of the greatest gifts of my career as a filmmaker. For nearly fifteen years we have seen how communities across the country and around the world have been inspired by the actions of people in Billings. Civic leaders, citizens, students and teachers have taken this story of resistance to hate and intolerance and made it their own.[5]

Jim Hunt, president of the National League of Cities, believes that one of the keys to opposing hate crimes is working to prevent them in the first place.

> We just can't wait until incidents happen. We have to be out there on a daily basis; we have to be working in communities; we have to be doing education. Personally, I think the power of the video is how we can get our messages out–if we don't use these resources, if we don't get out in front of that, we're just . . . asking for issues to come up.[6]

CONNECTIONS

How do you measure social change? What evidence would you look for? Why does social change often provoke a backlash? How might you respond to the backlash?

What does the story of Billings suggest about the way people can get involved? about the way one act leads to another and yet another? On what precedents did the people of Billings build? What legacies did they leave for their children? for other communities?

Police Chief Inman says that it took a long time for his "sense of social justice" to develop. What helped it to develop? How necessary is a "sense of social justice" to responsible citizenship in a democracy?

What does Anthony mean when she says, "We did something right here, and we will do it again if we have to. If we don't, there are people who would break every window in Billings, and we would look out those windows and see ourselves"? Marian Wright Edelman believes that "the good people's silence" can be "as damaging as the bad people's actions." Would Anthony agree? Do you agree?

What is a *hate crime*? What distinguishes a hate crime from other crimes? After a rock was thrown through the window of a home that belonged to a Vietnamese family, then-Deputy Superintendent William Johnston of the Boston Police Department noted that the rock did more than shatter glass; it also shattered a family. What do you think he means? How does this idea apply to what happened in Billings? (A video of Johnston's talk is available from the Facing History Resource Library.)

"Hate crimes are not a police problem," says former Police Chief Wayne Inman. "They're a community problem. Hate crimes and hate activity flourish only in communities that allow them to flourish." James Pace, the head of a racist "skinhead" group in Billings, agrees. He told a reporter, "If you have a racist problem, it was here and it's been here and it's going to be here if we are here or not." What do these comments suggest about the role of the bystander in a community? about the importance of how Billings or any other community defines its "universe of obligation"?

Why do you think people around the world have found this story so inspiring? How do stories inspire people to make a difference?

Fifteen years after the movement in Billings began, Not In Our Town (NIOT) Billings, a pro-diversity group that started after the 1994 incident and was revived in 2005, continues to meet once a month. NIOT Billings, whose motto is "moving our community from tolerance to acceptance," offers courses such as "Introduction to Diversity" and "Taking Action, Making Change," which provide guidelines on organizing communities to support racial justice. Since winter 2008 when a number of minority-owned restaurants were vandalized by white supremacist groups, NIOT Billings has held "eat-ins" where community-organized groups dine at the targeted businesses.

What do you think it takes to sustain a community movement? a national or international movement? Do these movements have anything in common, regardless of scale?

For examples of how different communities have used the Not In Our Town story as a model for change, go to *www.niot.org* or *www.choosingtoparticipate.org*.

 Watch this video:
www.facinghistory.org/video/not-our-town

---

[1] Claire Safran, "Not in Our Town," *Redbook*, November 1994.
[2] Roger Rosenblatt, "Their Finest Minute," *The New York Times*, July 3, 1994.
[3] Ibid.
[4] Ibid.
[5] Patrice O'Neill, email message to Adam Strom, June 16, 2009.
[6] Erika Gossert, email message to Adam Strom, June 12, 2009.

President John F. Kennedy once said that artists play a special role in a society. They contribute "not to our size [as a nation] but to our spirit; not to our political beliefs but to our insight; not to our self-esteem but to our self-comprehension."[1] Langston Hughes and Robert Frost are among the many American poets who have reflected on the choices we make as individuals and as citizens.

I Dream a World

by Langston Hughes

I dream a world where man
No other man will scorn,
Where love will bless the earth
And peace its paths adorn.
I dream a world where all
Will know sweet freedom's way,
Where greed no longer saps the soul
Nor avarice blights our day.
A world I dream where black or white,
Whatever race you be,
Will share the bounties of the earth
And every man is free,
Where wretchedness will hang its head,
And joy, like a pearl,
Attends the needs of all mankind.
Of such I dream, my world![2]

The Road Not Taken
by Robert Frost

Two roads diverged in a yellow wood,
And sorry I could not travel both
And be one traveler, long I stood
And looked down one as far as I could
To where it bent in the undergrowth;

Then took the other, as just as fair,
And having perhaps the better claim,
Because it was grassy and wanted wear;
Though as for that passing there
Had worn them really about the same,

And both that morning equally lay
In leaves no step had trodden black.
Oh, I kept the first for another day!
Yet knowing how way leads on to way,
I doubted if I should ever come back.

I shall be telling this with a sigh
Somewhere ages and ages hence:
Two roads diverged in a wood, and I–
I took the one less traveled by,
And that has made all the difference.[3]

CONNECTIONS

What is Langston Hughes's dream for the nation and the world? What democratic ideals are part of that dream? What part does democracy play in realizing that dream? How important is an honest confrontation with the past to realizing it? What is your dream for the nation and the world? What steps will you and others have to take to make it a reality?

Many say it is difficult to confront one's past when it reveals "bad things." For example, some politicians, educators, and parents believe that schools should not confront all of the nation's history. What do you think? What should schools teach about the nation's past?

When "two roads diverge," people are forced to make a choice. What is Frost suggesting about the importance of that choice? What is he suggesting about the difficulties in returning to make a different choice at a later time?

President Kennedy once said that a "nation which disdains the mission of art" invites the fate of the hired hand in one of Frost's most famous poems—"the fate of having nothing to look backward to with pride and nothing to look forward to with hope."[4] What is he suggesting about the relationship between past, present, and future?

What individuals you have encountered in your own life have taken the road "less traveled by," the one that "was grassy and wanted wear"? Did their choices make "all the difference"? How did those individuals help in some small or large way to make "a world where all/Will know sweet freedom's way"?

 Watch this video:
http://www.facinghistory.org/video/perception-jonathan-l-reads-his-poem

[1] President John F. Kennedy, "Remarks at Amherst College," October 26, 1963, John F. Kennedy Presidential Library & Museum, http://www.jfklibrary.org/ Historical+Resources/Archives/Reference+Desk/Speeches/ JFK/003POF03Amherst10261963.htm (accessed on August 7, 2007).

[2] Langston Hughes, " I Dream a World," *The Collected Poems of Langston Hughes*, edited by Arnold Rampersad (New York: Alfred A. Knopf, 2004), 311.

[3] Robert Frost, "The Road Not Taken," *Selected Poems of Robert Frost* (New York: Holt, Rinehart, and Winston, Inc.), 71–2.

[4] President John F. Kennedy, "Remarks at Amherst College," October 26, 1963.

For a fuller treatment of ideas developed in this guide, see *Facing History and Ourselves: Holocaust and Human Behavior.*

A variety of videos available from the Facing History Resource Center can be used to extend and enrich *Choosing to Participate.* Possibilities include: *Billings, MT: Not in Our Town; Eyes on the Prize: America's Civil Rights Years; Stand and Be Counted: Reacting to Racism; True Colors: Primetime Live.* See the Lending Library on the homepage of www.facinghistory.org for further information on these and other videos.

The following books can be used to explore specific topics and/or concepts:

Daisy Bates, *The Long Shadow of Little Rock* (Fayetteville: The University of Arkansas Press, 1997).

David Halberstam, *The Children* (New York: Random House, 1998).

Doris Kearns Goodwin, *Wait Till Next Year* (New York: Simon and Schuster, 1997).

Elizabeth Huckaby, *Crisis at Central High: Little Rock 1957–58* (Baton Rouge: Louisiana State University Press, 1980).

Marian Wright Edelman, *The Measure of Our Success: A Letter to My Children and Yours* (Boston: Beacon Press, 1992).

Melba Pattillo Beals, *Warriors Don't Cry: A Searing Memoir of the Battle to Integrate Little Rock's Central High* (New York: Pocket Books, 1994).

Phillip Hoose, *It's Our World, Too!* (New York: Farrar, Straus & Giroux, 2002).

Grateful acknowledgment is made for permission to reprint the following:

The centerpiece of the **CHOOSING TO PARTICIPATE** initiative is an interactive multimedia exhibition. Through the exploration of four stories from contemporary American history, visitors consider the central question, "What does it mean to be a citizen in a democracy?" These stories illustrate how democracy is a work in progress, shaped by the choices ordinary people and groups make about themselves and others—choices that form an individual, create a community, and ultimately forge a nation. **CHOOSING TO PARTICIPATE** helps visitors connect these stories to choices they face in their own lives through themes of identity, membership in society, what it means to be a newcomer, and the impact that difference has on a community and a nation.

CHOOSING TO

PARTICIPATE

The exhibition is comprised of four multimedia installations that illustrate the courage, initiative and compassion needed to protect democracy and human rights.

1. EVERYONE HAS A STORY describes the challenges of a child survivor of the Cambodian genocide and the people in his new community as he struggled to build a new life as a refugee in the United States.

2. LITTLE THINGS ARE BIG discusses a small but significant choice made during a late-night subway ride in New York City that illuminates how ideas about "race" influence the decisions people make about one another.

3. CRISIS IN LITTLE ROCK tells of the desegregation of a high school in 1957 and shows how courageous choices made by young people changed U.S. history and inspired others around the world.

4. NOT IN OUR TOWN shows how citizens of Billings, Montana, stood up for their neighbors in response to a series of hate crimes in their community.